Yes. I can Read, Write & Speak
Hindi Series.

LET'S BEGIN

Level I

By Rajiv Mahajan

Publisher

Buckskin Publishing Company
Columbia, Maryland, USA
hinditoday.com

Publisher:
Buckskin Publishing Company
Columbia, Maryland, USA
hinditoday.com

Price: US$ 25.00

Yes. I Can Read, Write & Speak Hindi Series
(Let's Begin) By Rajiv Mahajan
ISBN
$25.00
ISBN 978-0-615-56144-8
52500>
9 780615 561448

US Library Catalog Information

Design & Execution: NewLine Advertising and Marketing
Lead Designer: Naveen Kumar T. M.
Design support: V. R. Sunil Shastry
Special illustrations: B. B. Pattar

To My Dear Mom & Dad
with Love & Regards

CONTENTS

Objective of Book

The guiding light behind my endeavor to write this book as well as the philosophy that I have always lived my life by, has been the following quote from the Bhagavad Gita:

"Karmanye Vadhikaraste Ma Phaleshu Kadachana,
Ma Karma Phala Hetur Bhurmatey Sangostva Akarmani"
Which roughly translates to:

"You have a right to perform your prescribed action, but you are not entitled to the fruits of your action. Never consider yourself the cause of the results of your activities, and never be associated with not doing your duty."

Through this book it is my heartfelt desire and objective to make the entire process of learning Hindi fun and easy for the thousands of Indians that have settled in the United States or other parts of the world, who otherwise would have limited opportunity to adequately learn and imbibe our own language - Hindi. The entire exercise of learning should be one that parents and children alike, enjoy, rather than looking at it as a cumbersome and difficult exercise that has been thrust upon them. The initiative and the drive to learn the language should really come from within.

After reading this book series, parents and children alike, should themselves be able to sense the gap in their real knowledge, comfort and familiarity with the Hindi language. Irrespective of the part of India that they come from, especially if it is from a non-Hindi speaking background such as the southern states, this book series will give its readers a sense of understanding and overall confidence with the Hindi language.

Additionally, my observation over the years has been that although a lot of the Indians in the U.S. do know Hindi, they are hesitant to speak the same. I would like to see that hesitation, out through the window, and Indians across the US being able to speak in Hindi with a level of confidence and comfort that was hitherto unseen in the past.

This is the first book in the series 'Yes, I Can Read, Write and Speak Hindi.' After reading this book, children should be able to recognize the Hindi alphabet and letters with ease. From there they will gradually be able to decipher, read and frame 3-letter or 4-letter words which do not have the 'Matras'. If, for example, we take the alphabet 'क' (ka), the goal of this book series is to have your child read it, write it, understand it, and pronounce it correctly. Essentially, your child should be able to recognize individual alphabets, and then be able to join these letters together to form proper words, and eventually, complete sentences. That is when, real mastery over the Hindi language will actually occur for your child. Subsequent offerings in the 'Yes, I Can' series will act like building blocks on the foundation set in this first book. With each new book in the series, more words and techniques will be introduced to them to build a robust vocabulary of the Hindi language until they are eventually able to read, write, and converse in Hindi.

Words from the Author

This is my first novel attempt at writing a book, with the only goal being to teach Hindi and build an Attitude of 'Yes, I Can Read, Write and Speak Hindi.'

My entire inspiration for the book has come from the children whom I have been teaching. When I first started teaching, I strongly felt the need for a structured program in Hindi. The type of program that I envisioned was essentially missing. This would be a curriculum or material specifically targeted to children born in the United States. My observation has been that a lot of parents go to India on their summer vacations, and often pick up a book on learning Hindi at a local book store. When they get back, they put the book on the bookshelf and nothing happens and the book gathers dust! That book simply does not add any value whatsoever. Among the many reasons are the words and pictures that the kids see in those books. The book is written from an Indian perspective and there are images of people in traditional Indian attire. These are images that a lot of the kids in the U.S. simply cannot relate to. While some may scoff at my belief, I have found this to be reality. The fact is when they cannot connect with the picture, they lose interest in the book itself. Therefore, the attempt of this book is to keep children interested. The goal is to teach our children our own language, in a more localized or American way.

Keeping this aim in mind, I have not used literal words as used in Hindi which children in America are unlikely to have ever heard and so would probably never use either.

An additional observation that fueled the desire and ambition for this book was the fact that children in the U.S. already have a lot of school work and chores around the home which keeps them very busy. Considering the limited time that the children have to learn a new language on top of their normal school work, they need a fast paced platform to quickly learn and assimilate what is being taught. I feel that "generation Z" is growing up with the idea that things need to be communicated instantaneously. They are used to being catered to immediately and so the learning being imparted also has to be at the same pace.

In my opinion, the sequence of letters or alphabets in the Hindi language, are over emphasized by a lot of Hindi discourses and are simply irrelevant. The goal is to have the child read, write and speak Hindi. They are certainly not out to give a test or to get a degree in Hindi.

As a final note of inspiration for this book, I would also like to pay my fervent tribute to the Chinmaya Mission in Washington D.C. that I am a part of. The Mission has always been a great source of inspiration for me. Apart from the Mission, my own Swami Dheerananda Ji and of course my beloved parents, have both been major sources of inspiration for me, in my life.

Rajiv Mahajan

Acknowledgements and Dedications

At the outset, I dedicate this book to the early proponents of the Hindi language, a language which I am endeared to completely. It gives me a sense of identity and belief, which I find truly remarkable as well as inspirational.

Next, I wholeheartedly dedicate this book to my beloved students whom I had the privilege of teaching over the years, as well as all future students that I may never be able to teach personally. I am confident that this book series will make a positive difference to their lives. I am confident that this book will strike a chord with those children whose parents instill in them a positive attitude, and a sense of Yes I Can Read, Write and Speak Hindi.

I also dedicate this book to the Chinmaya Mission that I am a part of, one which has taught me so much in life.

No words of gratitude can ever be complete without acknowledging the contribution that my parents have made. By giving me an upbringing that always instilled in me the absolute desire to view life and its occurrences in a positive light.

I would also like to add a special note of thanks to those who made this book possible, as you currently see it in its physical form, through various suggestions, comments, allegories, pictures, and their own words. In particular, I would like to thank:

My mother-in-law, Shrimati Sudarshan Mahajan, whose suggestions for the book were simply invaluable.

My beloved wife, Shalini Gupta, who has stood by my side no matter what was happening around us. She is a steadfast rock in good and bad times alike. The book would have been impossible without her cooperation and understanding.

Without magical strokes with the digital artistic brush of a young team, this book would never really have felt and seemed as visually appealing as it currently is.

I would like to sincerely thank creative team, for exquisitely crafting a lot of my thoughts to words that simply spelt magic – thank you!

Ultimately, as with most situations in life, it is all about teamwork, and it is this very teamwork, with all of the aforementioned individuals and many more, that has successfully resulted in having this book see the light of day, and my being able to say – 'Yes, I Can'!

Before I conclude, I would like to add a few words which the legendary basketball player, Michael Jordan once said on teamwork: "Talent wins games, but teamwork and intelligence wins championships".

My effort with this book is that you win the championship of learning Hindi, fervently, with a resounding 'Yes I Can' attitude! That is where I feel my goals will truly be achieved.

- Rajiv Mahajan

INTRODUCTION

Let's step into the amazing new world !

Vowels

अ	आ	इ	ई	उ	ऊ	ए	ऐ	ओ	औ	अं	अः
a	ā	i	ī	u	ū	e	ai	o	au	ń, ḿ	Half-h
Short Vowel	Long Vowel	Short Vowel	Long Vowel	Short Vowel	Long Vowel	Short Vowel	Long Vowel	Short Vowel	Long Vowel		
	◌ा	◌ि	◌ी	◌ु	◌ू	◌े	◌ै	◌ो	◌ौ	◌ं	◌ः
						One flag	Two flags	One flag with one stem	Two flags with one stem		

Consonants

क	ख	ग	घ	ङ
ka	kha	ga	gha	ńga

च	छ	ज	झ	ञ
cha	chha	ja	jha, za	ña

ट	ठ	ड	ढ	ण
ṭa	ṭha	ḍa	ḍha	ṇa

त	थ	द	ध	न
ta	tha	da	dha	na

प	फ	ब	भ	म
pa	pha, fa	ba	bha	ma

य	र	ल	व
ya	ra	La	va, wa

श	ष	स	ह
sha	ṣha	sa	ha

क्ष	त्र	ज्ञ
kṣha	tra	gya

Vowels

Full Form		Sounds Like	As In	Abbreviated form (Matras)
अ *	अ	a Short Vowel	America	——
आ	आ	ā Long Vowel	Car	◌ा
इ	इ	i Short Vowel	Pin	ि◌
ई	ई	ī Long Vowel	Feet	◌ी
उ	उ	u Short Vowel	Put	◌ु
ऊ	ऊ	ū Long Vowel	Moon	◌ू
ए	ए	e Short Vowel	Play	◌े One flag
ऐ	ऐ	ai Long Vowel	High	◌ै Two flags
ओ	ओ	o Short Vowel	Go	◌ो One flag with one stem
औ	औ	au Long Vowel	Count	◌ौ Two flags with one stem
अं	अं	ń, ḿ	Come	◌ं
अः	अः	Half-h	Ah	◌ः

* Vowel अ (a) is inherent vowel in all consonant when no other vowel is present.
Vowel अ (a) is silent for last consonant in a word.

Consonants

Consonant		Sounds Like	As In
क	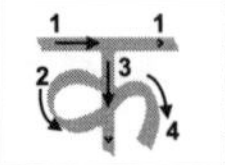	ka	milk
ख	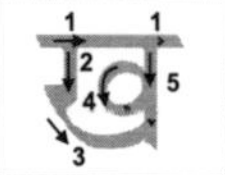	kha	khaki
ग	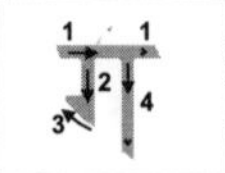	ga	gate
घ		gha	ghost
ङ		ńga	bring
च		cha	charm
छ		chha (ć with breath)	Match
ज		ja	jug
झ		jha	dodge
ञ	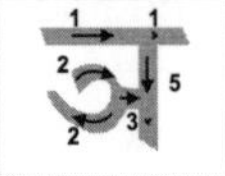	ñа	buñch
ट		ṭa	cuṭ
ठ		ṭha	ṭhug
ड	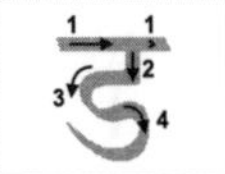	ḍa	ḍirt
ढ		ḍha	aḍhere
ण	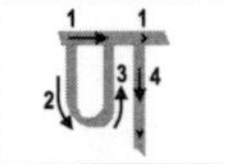	ṇa	baṇd
त	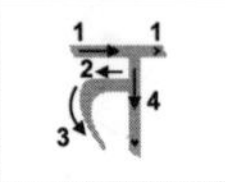	ta	tapir (close to think)
थ		tha	thunder

Consonant		Sounds Like	As In
द	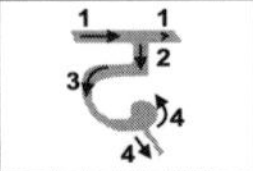	da	other (close to father)
ध	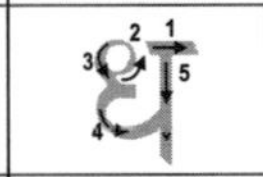	dha	buddha
न	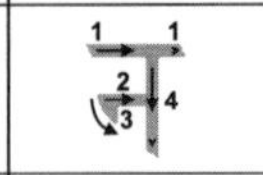	na	men
प	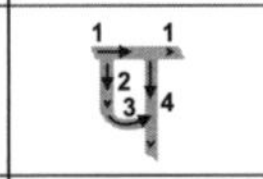	pa	cup
फ	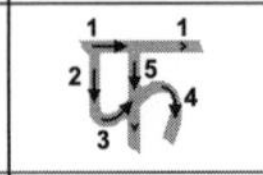	pha, fa	photo, fan
ब	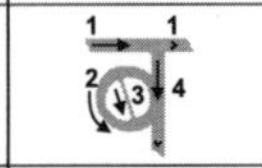	ba	balloon
भ	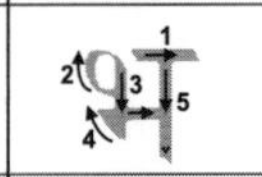	bha	bharal
म	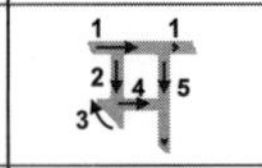	ma	mug
य	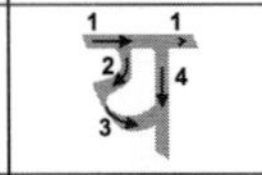	ya	yes
र	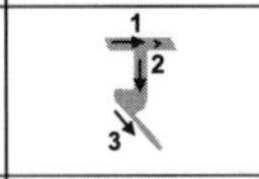	ra	run
ल	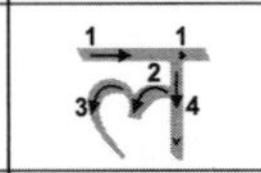	La	Love
व	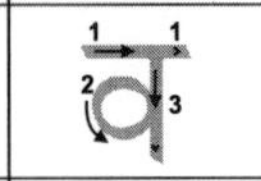	va, wa	rave, watch
श	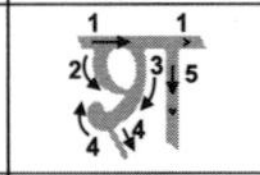	sha	shell
ष	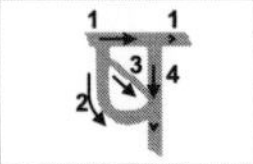	ṣha	ṣhut
स	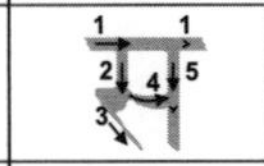	sa	sun
ह	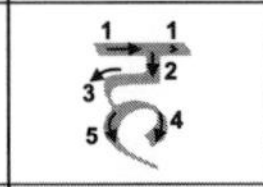	ha	hug
क्ष	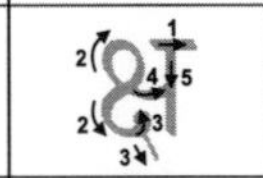	kṣha	workṣheet
त्र	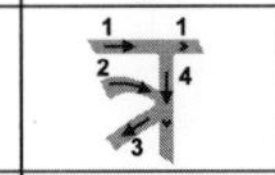	tra	thrash (close to three)
ज्ञ	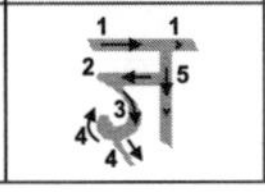	gya	harangue

Consonants in Random Order

	ब	स	न	ल	घ	र	क
	म	ह	च	द	व	ख	ज
	प	थ	त	ग	ट	य	ड
	श	ध	ङ	झ	भ	छ	फ
ढ	ठ	ष	ण	क्ष	त्र	ज्ञ	ञ

Vowels - Full Form in Random Order

अ ई उ ए आ इ

अः ऊ ओ ऐ औ अं

Matras - Abbreviated Form in Random Order

◌ा ि◌ ◌ु ◌े ◌ी ◌ो

◌ू ◌ै ◌ौ ◌ः ◌ं

Learn to Pronounce Hindi Characters

✓*													
		अ a	आ ā ◌ा	इ i ि◌	ई ī ◌ी	उ u ◌ु	ऊ ū ◌ू	ए e ◌े	ऐ ai ◌ै	ओ o ◌ो	औ au ◌ौ	अं ń, ḿ ◌ं	अः Half-h ◌ः
	ka	क ka	का kā	कि ki	की kī	कु ku	कू kū	के ke	कै kai	को ko	कौ kau	कं kń,kḿ	कः kh
	kha	ख	खा	खि	खी	खु	खू	खे	खै	खो	खौ	खं	खः
	ga	ग	गा	गि	गी	गु	गू	गे	गै	गो	गौ	गं	गः
	gha	घ	घा	घि	घी	घु	घू	घे	घै	घो	घौ	घं	घः
	cha	च	चा	चि	ची	चु	चू	चे	चै	चो	चौ	चं	चः
	chha	छ	छा	छि	छी	छु	छू	छे	छै	छो	छौ	छं	छः
	ja	ज	जा	जि	जी	जु	जू	जे	जै	जो	जौ	जं	जः
	jha, za	झ	झा	झि	झी	झु	झू	झे	झै	झो	झौ	झं	झः
	ṭa	ट	टा	टि	टी	टु	टू	टे	टै	टो	टौ	टं	टः
	ṭha	ठ	ठा	ठि	ठी	ठु	ठू	ठे	ठै	ठो	ठौ	ठं	ठः
	ḍa	ड	डा	डि	डी	डु	डू	डे	डै	डो	डौ	डं	डः
	ḍha	ढ	ढा	ढि	ढी	ढु	ढू	ढे	ढै	ढो	ढौ	ढं	ढः
	ṇa	ण	णा	णि	णी	णु	णू	णे	णै	णो	णौ	णं	णः
	ta	त	ता	ति	ती	तु	तू	ते	तै	तो	तौ	तं	तः
	tha	थ	था	थि	थी	थु	थू	थे	थै	थो	थौ	थं	थः
	da	द	दा	दि	दी	दु	दू	दे	दै	दो	दौ	दं	दः
	dha	ध	धा	धि	धी	धु	धू	धे	धै	धो	धौ	धं	धः

*Put a check mark inside the box after learning the respective Consonants & Vowels.

Learn to Pronounce Hindi Characters

☑*		☐	☐	☐	☐	☐	☐	☐	☐	☐	☐	☐	☐
		अ a	आ ā ◌ा	इ i ि◌	ई ī ◌ी	उ u ◌ु	ऊ ū ◌ू	ए e ◌े	ऐ ai ◌ै	ओ o ◌ो	औ au ◌ौ	अं ń, ḿ ◌ं	अः Half-h ◌ः
☐	na	न	ना	नि	नी	नु	नू	ने	नै	नो	नौ	नं	नः
☐	pa	प	पा	पि	पी	पु	पू	पे	पै	पो	पौ	पं	पः
☐	pha, fa	फ	फा	फि	फी	फु	फू	फे	फै	फो	फौ	फं	फः
☐	ba	ब	बा	बि	बी	बु	बू	बे	बै	बो	बौ	बं	बः
☐	bha	भ	भा	भि	भी	भु	भू	भे	भै	भो	भौ	भं	भः
☐	ma	म	मा	मि	मी	मु	मू	मे	मै	मो	मौ	मं	मः
☐	ya	य	या	यि	यी	यु	यू	ये	यै	यो	यौ	यं	यः
☐	ra	र	रा	रि	री	रु	रू	रे	रै	रो	रौ	रं	रः
☐	La	ल	ला	लि	ली	लु	लू	ले	लै	लो	लौ	लं	लः
☐	va, wa	व	वा	वि	वी	वु	वू	वे	वै	वो	वौ	वं	वः
☐	sha	श	शा	शि	शी	शु	शू	शे	शै	शो	शौ	शं	शः
☐	ṣha	ष	षा	षि	षी	षु	षू	षे	षै	षो	षौ	षं	षः
☐	sa	स	सा	सि	सी	सु	सू	से	सै	सो	सौ	सं	सः
☐	ha	ह	हा	हि	ही	हु	हू	हे	है	हो	हौ	हं	हः
☐	kṣha	क्ष	क्षा	क्षि	क्षी	क्षु	क्षू	क्षे	क्षै	क्षो	क्षौ	क्षं	क्षः
☐	tra	त्र	त्रा	त्रि	त्री	त्रु	त्रू	त्रे	त्रै	त्रो	त्रौ	त्रं	त्रः
☐	gya	ज्ञ	ज्ञा	ज्ञि	ज्ञी	ज्ञु	ज्ञू	ज्ञे	ज्ञौ	ज्ञो	ज्ञौ	ज्ञं	ज्ञः

*Put a check mark inside the box after learning the respective Consonants & Vowels.

Vowels

अ	अदरक	Ginger	ए	एड़ी	Heel
आ	आम	Mango	ऐ	ऐनक	Glasses
इ	इतवार	Sunday	ओ	ओम	Om
ई	ईशवर	God	औ	औरत	Woman
उ	उंगली	Finger	अं	अंगूर	Grapes
ऊ	ऊपर	Up	अः **	पुनः	Again

Consonants

क	केला	Banana	ड	ड़ाकिया	Postman	म	मछली	Fish
ख	खरगोश	Rabbit	ढ	ढोल	Drum	य	योगा	Yoga
ग	गाजर	Carrot	ण **	दक्षिण	South direction	र	रोटी	Bread
घ	घोड़ा	Horse	त	तारा	Star	ल	लाल	Red
ङ **	मंगलवार	Tuesday	थ	थैला	Bag	व	वीरवार	Thursday
च	चम्मच	Spoon	द	दाड़ी	Beard	श	शनिवार	Saturday
छ	छतरी	Umbrella	ध	धागा	Thread	ष	षटकोण	Hexagon
ज	जूता	Shoe	न	नाखून	Nail	स	सोमवार	Monday
झ	झाड़ू	Broom	प	पतंग	Kite	ह	हाथी	Elephant
ञ **	मंदिर	Temple	फ	फल	Fruit	क्ष	पक्षी	Bird
ट	टमाटर	Tomato	ब	बुधवार	Wednesday	त्र	त्रिभुज	Triangle
ठ	ठप्पा	To put stamp	भ	भालू	Bear	ज्ञ	ज्ञान	Knowledge

Word and Sentence Formation

म + ए | र + आ | न + आ | म | र + आ | ज + आ | ह + ऐ → Consonants & vowels in full form

↓ ↓

म + े | र + ा | न + ा | म | र + ा | ज + ा | ह + ै → Consonants & vowels in abbreviated form

मे रा | ना म | रा जा | है → Joining consonants & vowels

मेरा | नाम | राजा | है → Forming words

मेरा नाम राजा है । → Forming sentence

merā nām rājā hai

My name is Raja.

** Hollow letters, usually are not beginning sounds only in conjucts.

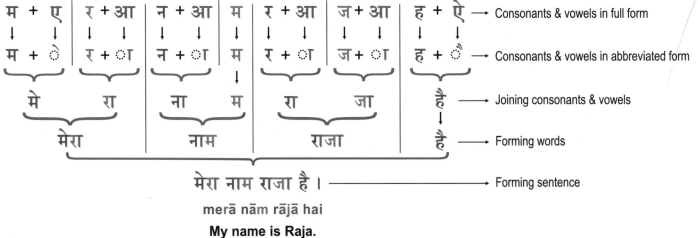

Hey I like this !
It is very interesting !

LESSON-1

It feels good to learn Hindi !

Letters

न

(na) men

म

(ma) mug

ग

(ga) gate

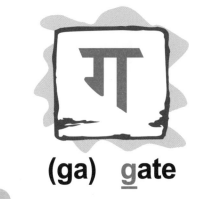

Letter Writing

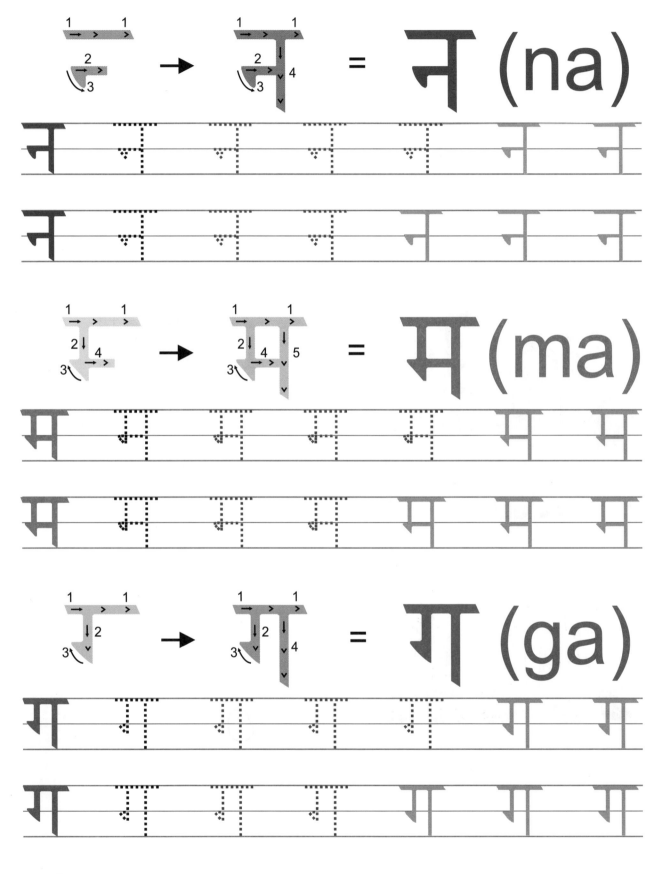

= न (na)

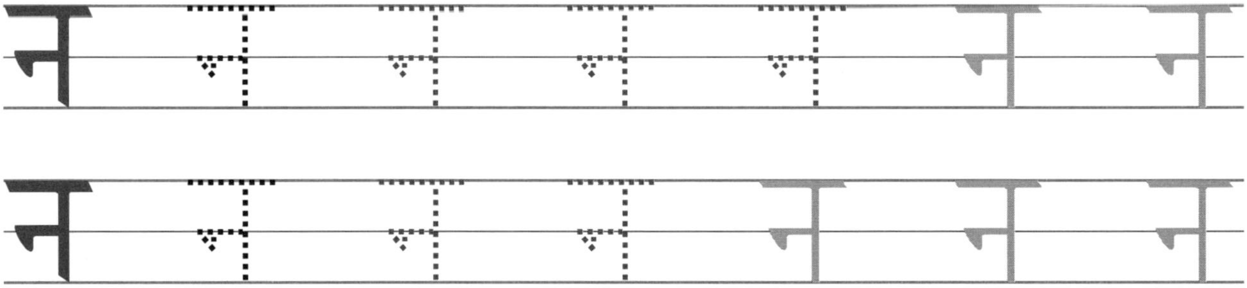

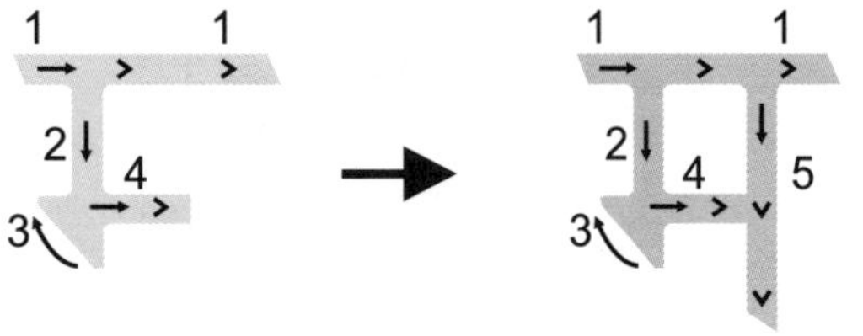

= म (ma)

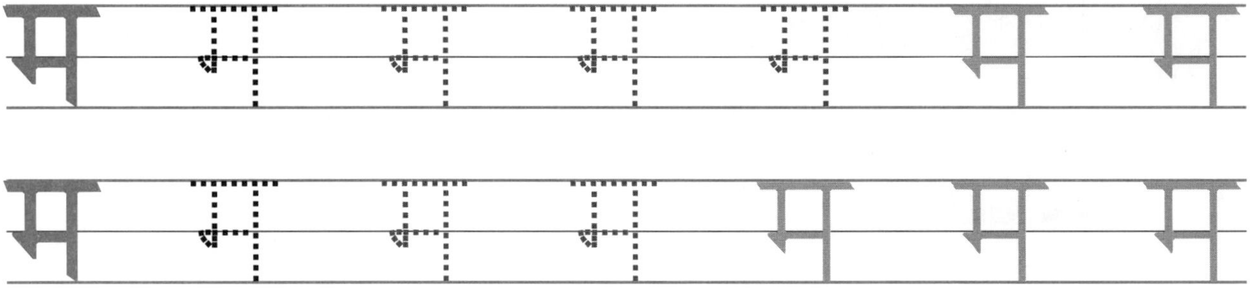

= ग (ga)

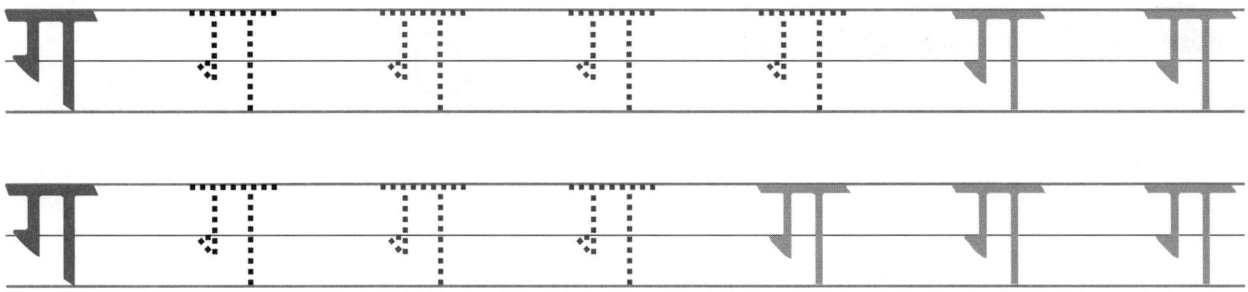

Hindi Word Building

ग	+	न	=	गन	→	ग	+	न	+	ग	=	गनग
ga	+	n	=	gan	→	ga	+	na	+	g	=	ganag
म	+	न	=	मन	→	म	+	न	+	ग	=	मनग
ma	+	n	=	man	→	ma	+	na	+	g	=	manag
म	+	ग	=	मग	→	म	+	ग	+	न	=	मगन
ma	+	g	=	mag	→	ma	+	ga	+	n	=	magan
न	+	ग	=	नग	→	न	+	ग	+	म	=	नगम
na	+	g	=	nag	→	na	+	ga	+	m	=	nagam

Build the following words

न + म = ______

म + न = ______

म + ग = ______

ग + म = ______

न + म + न = ______

म + न + ग = ______

म + ग + न = ______

ग + म + न = ______

न + म + न + म = ______

म + ग + न + ग = ______

Combine the letters to form words

Example: na + m → न + म = नम

na + g = ______

ga + n = ______

ma + n = ______

ga + m = ______

ma + g = ______

ma + m = ______

na + m = ______

na + n = ______

ga + g = ______

Word Meaning

गन → gun → Gun

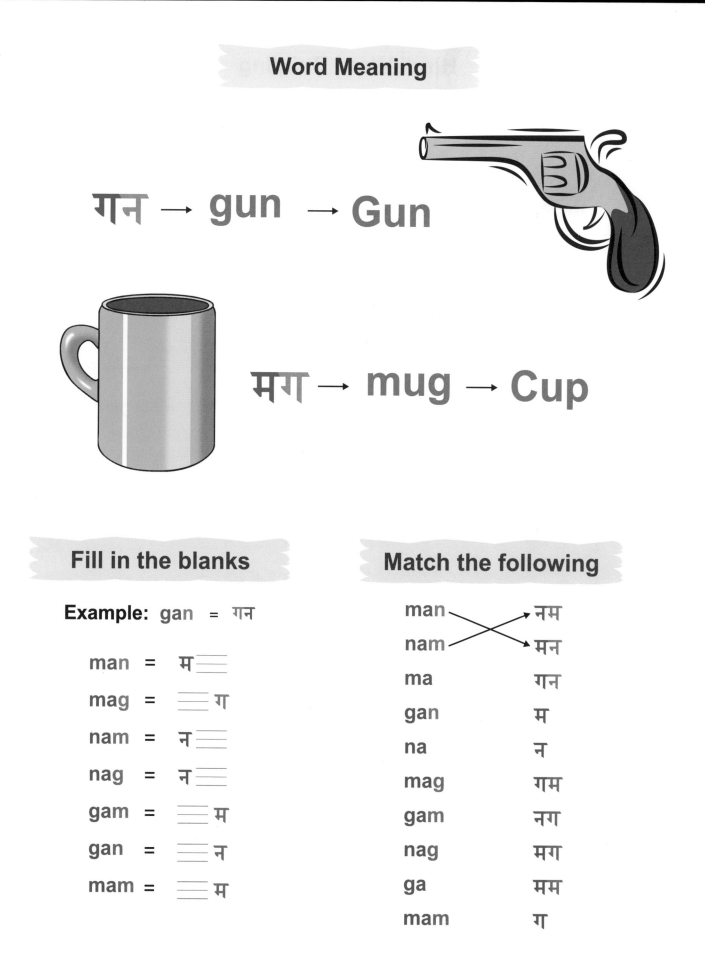

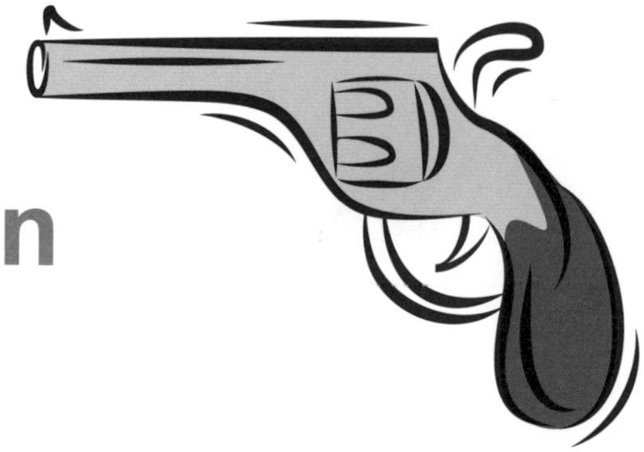

मग → mug → Cup

Fill in the blanks

Example: gan = गन

man = म ___

mag = ___ ग

nam = न ___

nag = न ___

gam = ___ म

gan = ___ न

mam = ___ म

Match the following

man	नम
nam	मन
ma	गन
gan	म
na	न
mag	गम
gam	नग
nag	मग
ga	मम
mam	ग

That was quite easy !

Go to page 6-7 and check in the box.

LESSON-2

It is not going to be tough !

Letters

व

(va,wa) watch

ब

(ba) balloon

क

(ka) milk

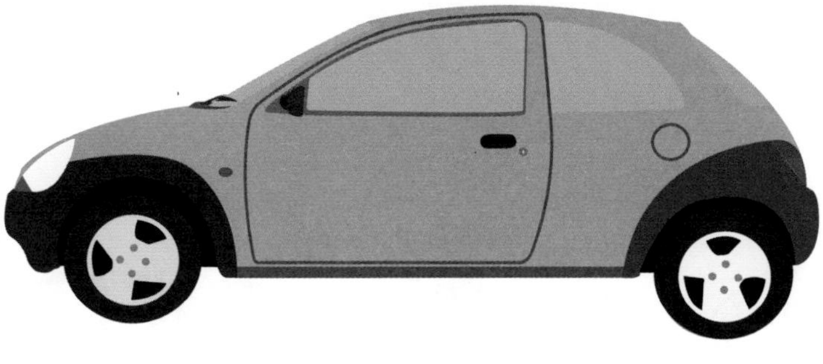

आ

ा

(ā) cār

			Vowel	Vowel Sign	Sounds Like	
व	va,wa	watch	आ	ा	ā	वा
ब	ba	balloon	आ	ा	ā	बा
क	ka	milk	आ	ा	ā	का

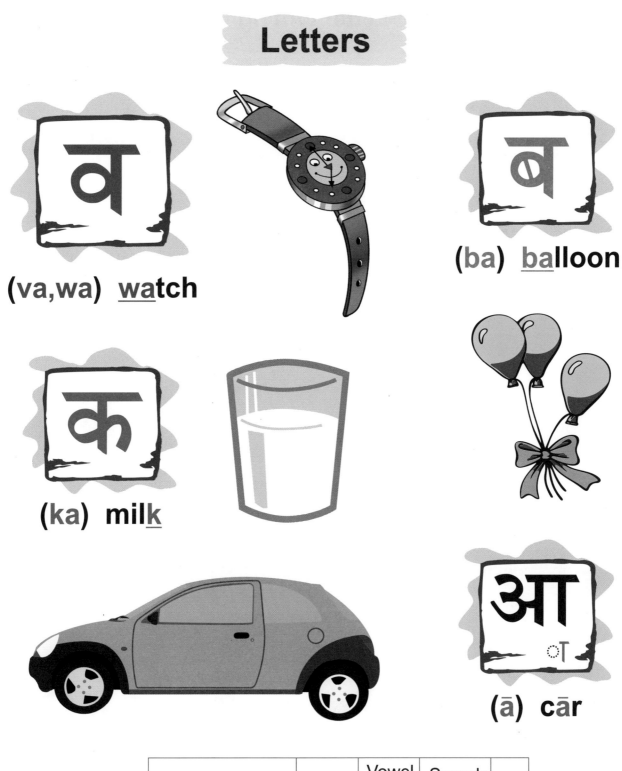

दो Do

Letter Writing

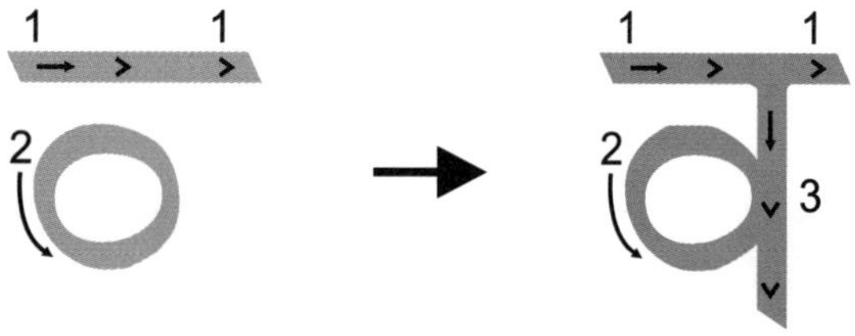

= व (va)

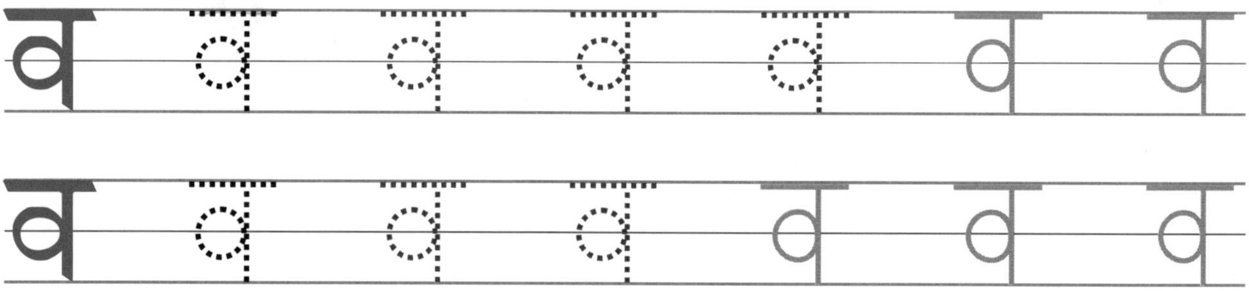

= ब (ba)

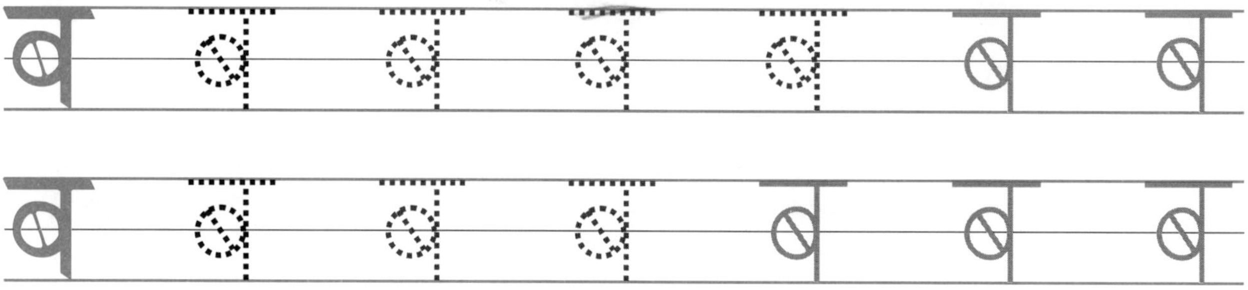

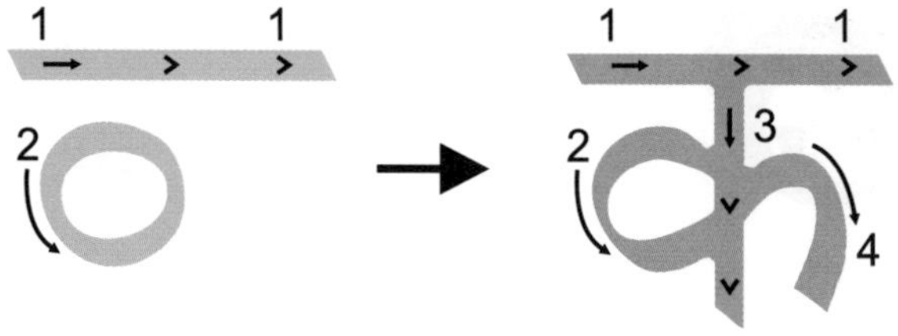

= क (ka)

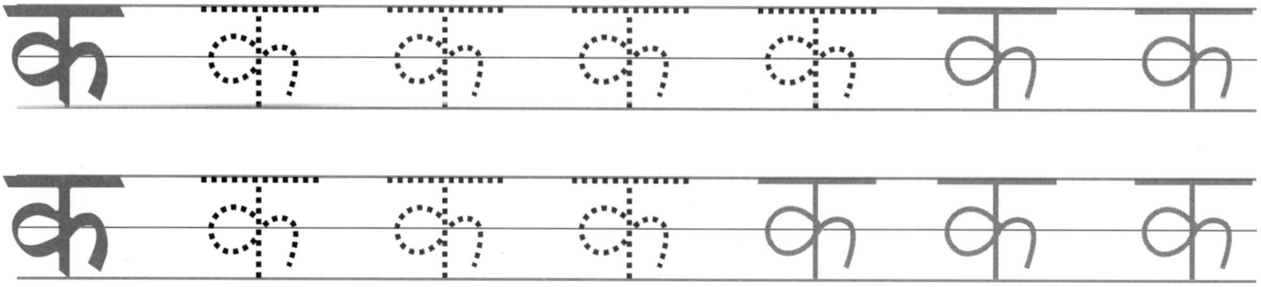

दो Do

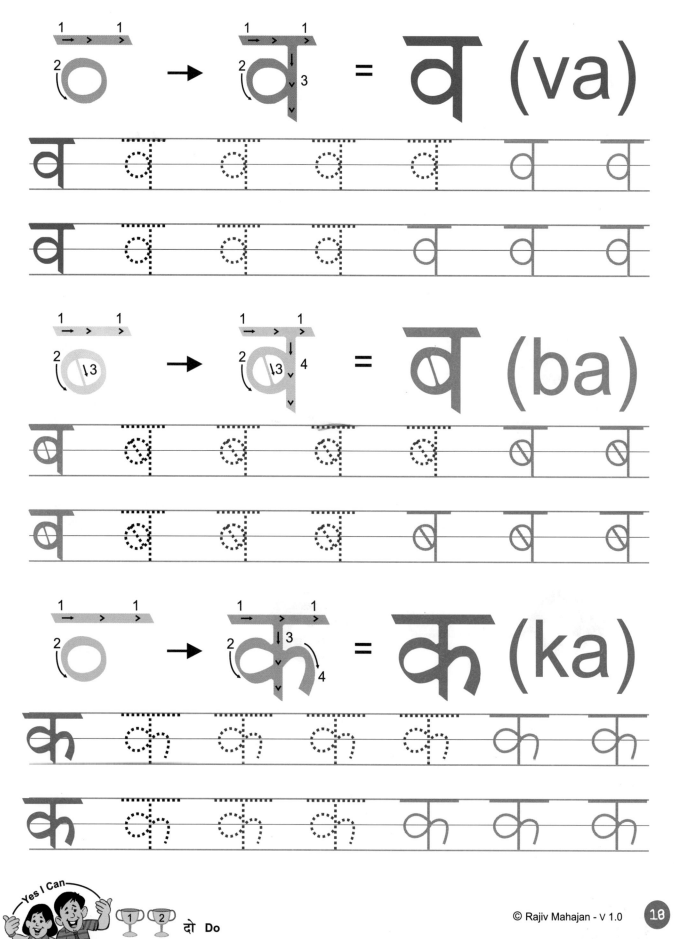

Hindi Word Building

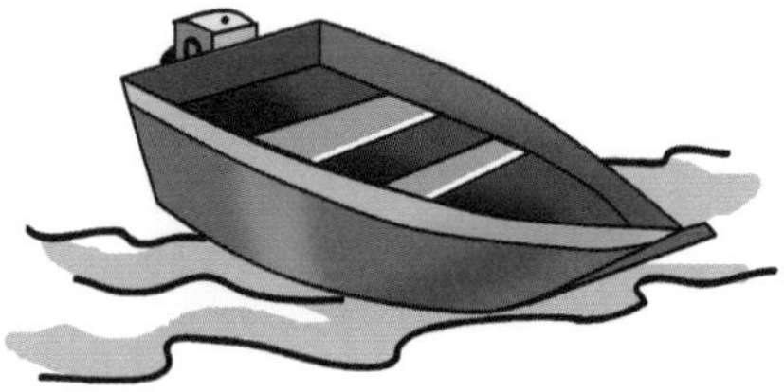

न + ◌ा = ना

न + ◌ा + व = नाव

na + ā + v = nāv **(Boat)**

न + ◌ा = ना

न + ◌ा + म = नाम

na + ā + m = nām **(Name)**

क + ◌ा = का

क + ◌ा + म = काम

ka + ā + m = kām **(Work)**

क + ◌ा = का

क + ◌ा + क + ◌ा = काका

ka + ā + ka + ā = kākā **(Elder Brother)**

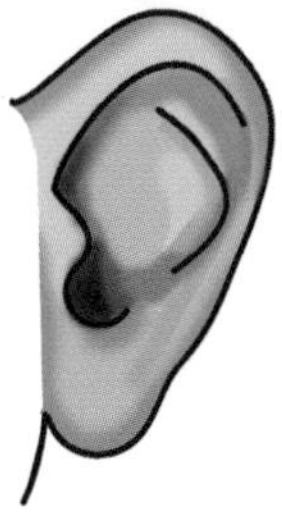

क + ◌ा = का

क + ◌ा + न = कान

ka + ā + n = kān **(Ear)**

न + ◌ा = ना

न + ◌ा + न + ◌ा = नाना

na + ā + na + ā = nānā **(Maternal Grand Father)**

Build the following words

ब + क = ________   बा + ग = ________

न + व = ________   ना + ना = ________

म + क = ________   मा + मा = ________

व + न = ________   ना + म = ________

ब + न = ________   का + न = ________

न + म + क = ________

क + न + क = ________

Combine the letters to form words

Example: ba + k = बक

ka + b = ________   nā + m = ________

na + b = ________   ka + v = ________

va + k = ________   kā + n = ________

ma + k = ________   nā + k = ________

kā + m = ________   ka + m = ________

va + v = ________

Want to try some juicy stuff?

तरबूज tarabūj **Watermelon**

Word Meaning

कब → kab → When

When are you visiting my home?

नाक → nāk → Nose

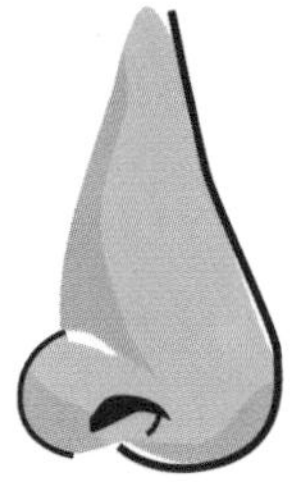

वन → van → Forest

मकान → makān → House

मानव → mānav → Human

नमक → namak → Salt

SALT
SALT SALT SALT

कम → kam → Less

बाग → bāg → Garden

Fill in the blanks

Example: bak = बक

kab	=	क ___	kav	=	___ व
nāv	=	___ व	kān	=	___ न
van	=	___ न	ban	=	ब ___
kām	=	___ म	nab	=	न ___
vak	=	व ___	kām	=	___ म

Match the following

bak	कब	nab	बन
kab	बक	ban	ब
van	काम	ba	नब
kām	वन	kān	न
nāv	क	na	व
ka	नाव	va	कान

Let's splash a bit of color!

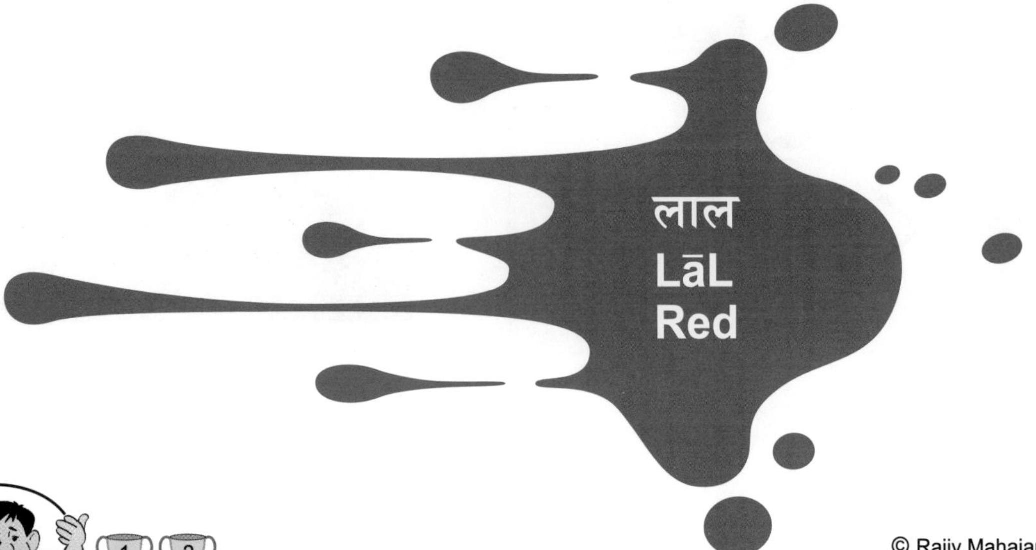

Reading

न	म	ग	ब	व	क
na	ma	ga	ba	va	ka

आ
ा
ā

कम, गम, नम, मन, गन, बन, वन

नग, मग, बक, वक, कब, अब

नमक, कनक, गमक, बनक, मनक

नमन, गमन, वमन, गगन, मगन

नाम, काम, बाम, वाम, गाम, आम

कान, मान, गान, बान, नाव

नाक, वाक, बाक, काक, गाक

नाना, मामा, बाबा, काका, माना, आना

मकान, बगान, कमान, बनाम,

बामन, नानक, नामक, कामना, बकना

बनना, मानना, बनाना, कमाना, गवाना

गाना गा। मकान बना। वन बना।

नाम कमा। काम बना। कब बना।

See I told you it wasn't tough !

Don't forget to check on page 6-7

LESSON-3

Ah ! A new chapter !

Letters

त

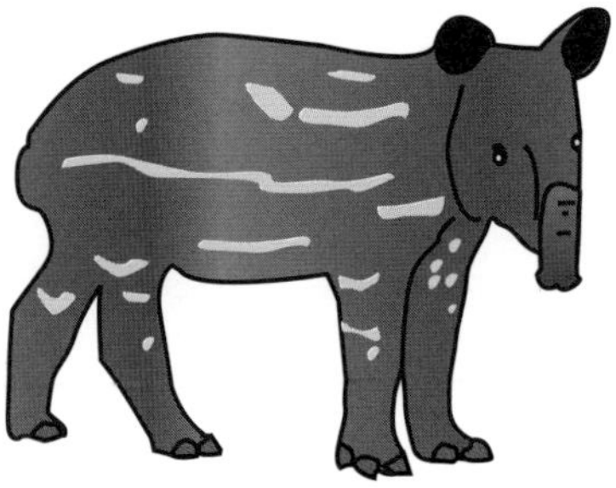

भ

(ta) tapir
(Close to think)

(bha) bharal

प

(pa) cup

इ ि

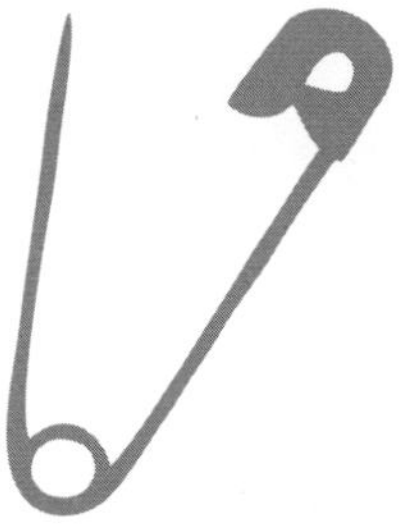

ई ी

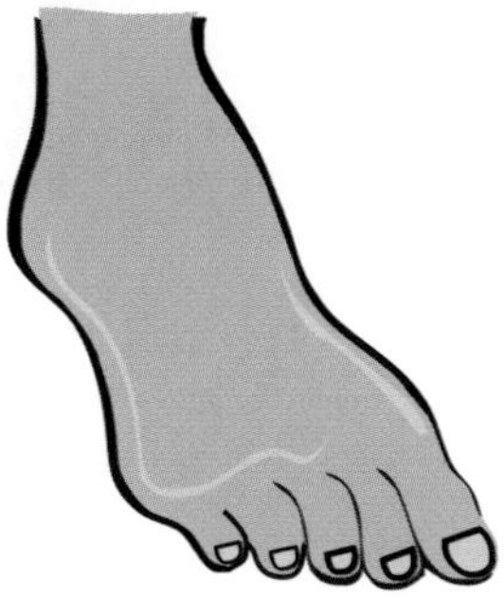

(i) pin

(ī) feet

			Vowel	Vowel Sign	Sounds Like		
त	ta	tapir	इ, ई	◌ि ◌ी	i, ī	ति, ती	ti, tī
भ	bha	bharal	इ, ई	◌ि ◌ी	i, ī	भि, भी	bhi, bhī
प	pa	cup	इ, ई	◌ि ◌ी	i, ī	पि, पी	pi, pī

Letter Writing

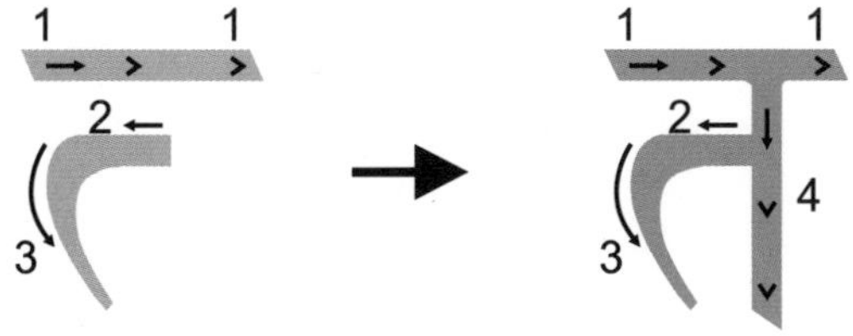

= त (ta)

त

त

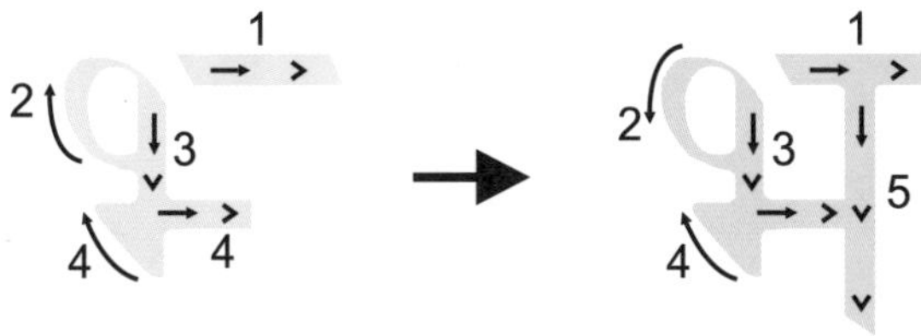

= भ (bha)

भ

भ

= प (pa)

प

प

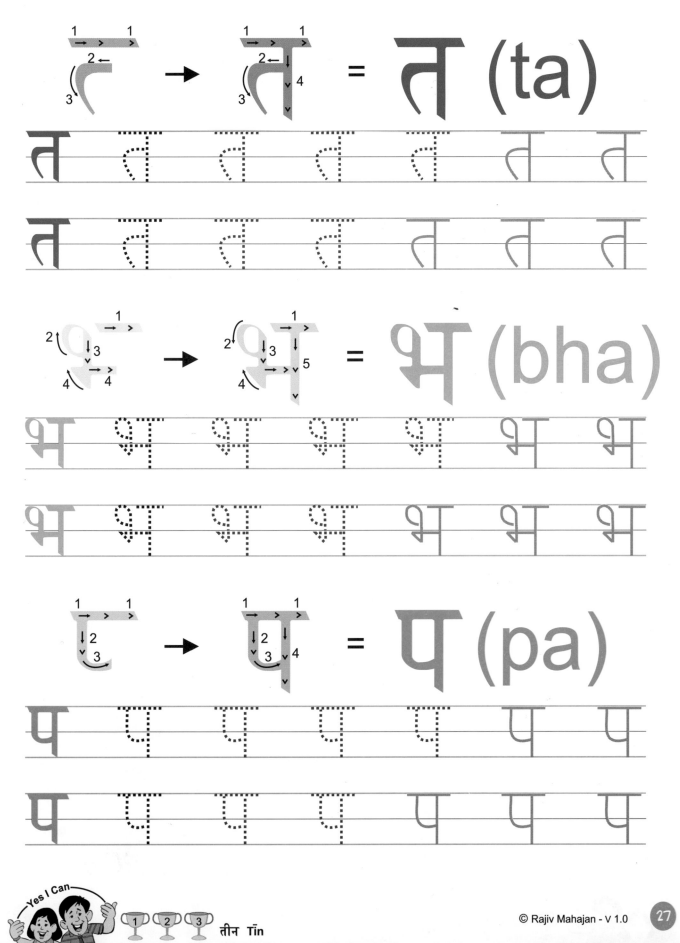

Hindi Word Building

ि + त = ति

प + ति = पति

pa + ti = pati **(Husband)**

ि + प = पि

पि + न = पिन

pi + n = pin **(Pin)**

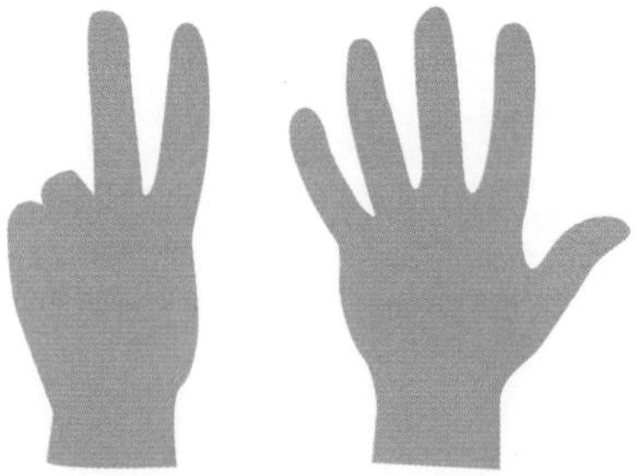

ि + ग = गि

न + ा = ना

गि + न + ना = गिनना

gi + na + nā = ginanā **(Count)**

प + ा = पा

न + ी = नी

पा + नी = पानी

pā + nī = pānī **(Water)**

भ + ी = भी

न + ा = ना

भी + ग + ना = भीगना

bhī + ga + nā = bhīganā **(Getting Wet)**

प + (प + ी) + (त + ा)

प + पी + ता = पपीता

pa + pī + tā = papītā **(Papaya)**

तीन Tīn

Build the following words

पि + ता = ______

नी + म = ______

गि + न = ______

वी + क = ______

ना + प = ______

गी + ता = ______

ति + न + का = ______

ती + न = ______

Combine the letters to form words

Example: **pi** + tā = पिता

pi + n = ______

bhā + p = ______

mī + nā = ______

nā + p + **nā** = ______

mā + tā = ______

tī + n = ______

gi + na + **nā** = ______

bhī + ga + **nā** = ______

kī + ma + **t** = ______

pa + pī + **tā** = ______

Let's hunt for colors in Hindi!

नीला niLā Blue

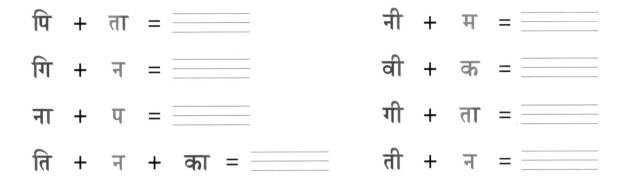

Word Meaning

नाप → nāp → **Measure**

गीता → gītā
Name/Holy Book

भाप → bhāp → **Steam**

कीमत → kīmat → **Price**

भवन → bhavan → **House**

वतन → vatan → **Country**

USA →

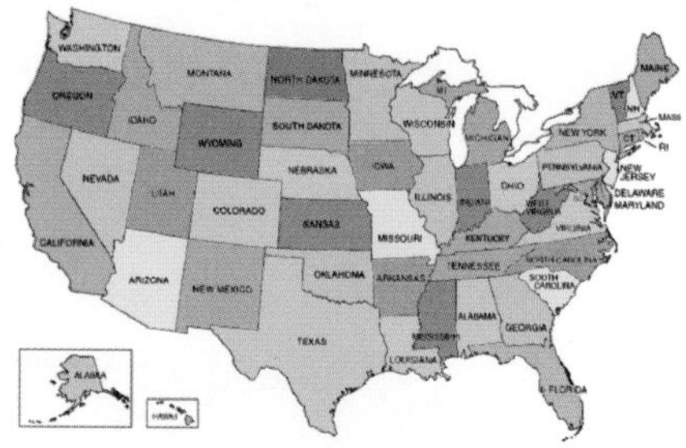

माता–पिता
mātā-pitā → **Parents**

तीन → tīn → **Three**

Fill in the blanks

Example: pā + ni = पानी

pi	+ n	=	____ न	bhā	+ p	=	____ प
mī	+ nā	=	____ ना	nā + pa	+ nā	=	नाप ____
pā	+ p	=	____ प	pa + pī	+ tā	=	प ____ ता
pī	+ nā	=	____ ना	bha + va	+ n	=	भ ____
gī	+ tā	=	____ ता	gi + na	+ nā	=	____ ना

Match the following

pīnā	पानी	gītā	भीगना
pānī	पीना	mātā	गीता
pitā	तीन	bhīgnā	माता
nāp	पिता	bahvan	पपीता
tīn	मीना	papītā	पिन
mīnā	नाप	pin	भवन

Let's bite into some fruits!

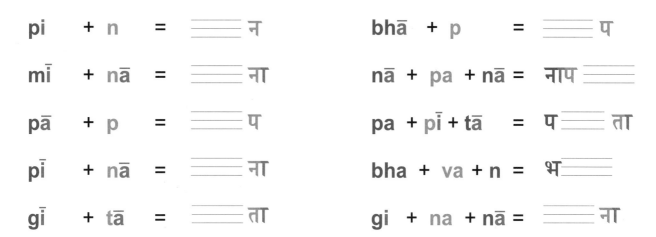

Reading

न	म	ग	ब	व	क	त	भ	प
na	ma	ga	ba	va	ka	ta	bha	pa

आ	इ	ई
◌ा	◌ि	◌ी
ā	i	ī

नाग, बाग, भाग, बात, भात, मात, भाप

गीता, मीता, नीता, पीता, तीन, बीन, नीम

किन, बिन, गिन, नित, बिग, पिन

पापी, बानी, पानी, नानी, वानी

मानव, पावन, बगान, भागना

कमान, भावना, नापना, अपना

माता–पिता, नाना–नानी, काका–काकी, मामा–मामी

विमान, कितना, बबीता, निकिता, नमिता

बात मान। भाग मत। पानी पी। अब गाना गा।

भीग मत। गिनती गिन। तीन तक गिन।

गीता भीग मत। मीना अपना नाम बता।

चपाती बना। पता बता। कीमत बता।

माता–पिता की बात मान। वचन मान।

तपन, भवन, वचन, पतन, भनक

अपना काम बता। बाकी काम बता।

Hey man ! I have done it !

Go to page 6-7 and check

LESSON-4

Keep going you are doing well !

Letters

च

छ

(cha) charm

(chha) C' with breath
(Match)

ज

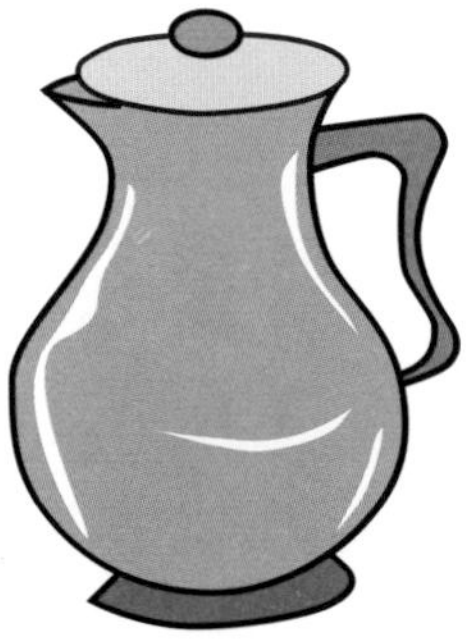

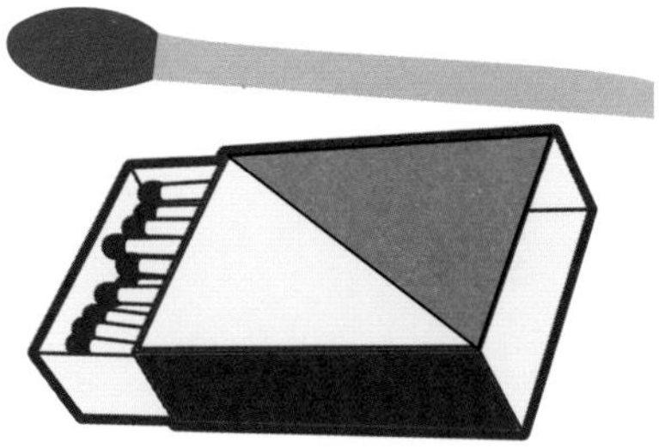

(ja) Jug

उ ु

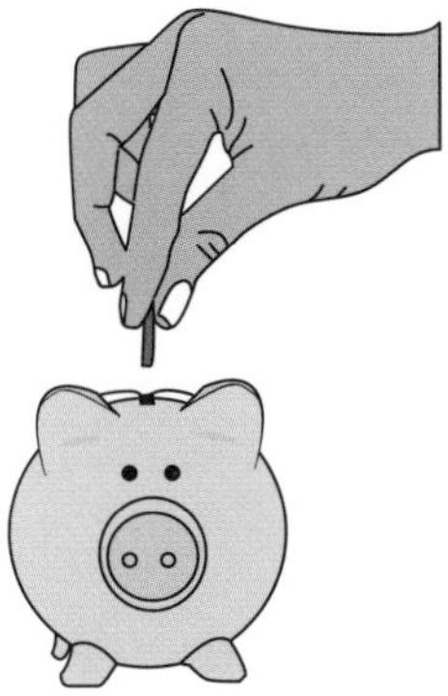

ऊ ू

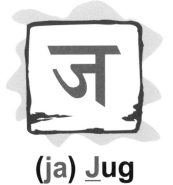

(u) put

(ū) moon

			Vowel	Sounds Like	Vowel Sign		
च	cha	charm	उ, ऊ	u, ū	ु ू	चु, चू	chu, chū
छ	chha	C' with breath	उ, ऊ	u, ū	ु ू	छु, छू	chhu, chhū
ज	ja	jug	उ, ऊ	u, ū	ु ू	जु, जू	ju, jū

Letter Writing

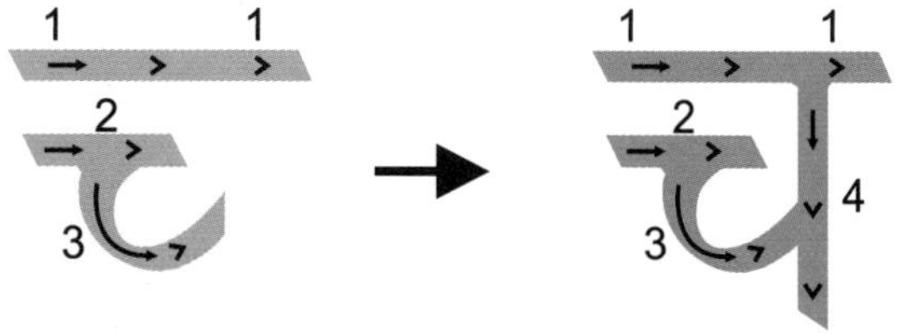

= च (cha)

च

च

= छ (chha)

छ

छ

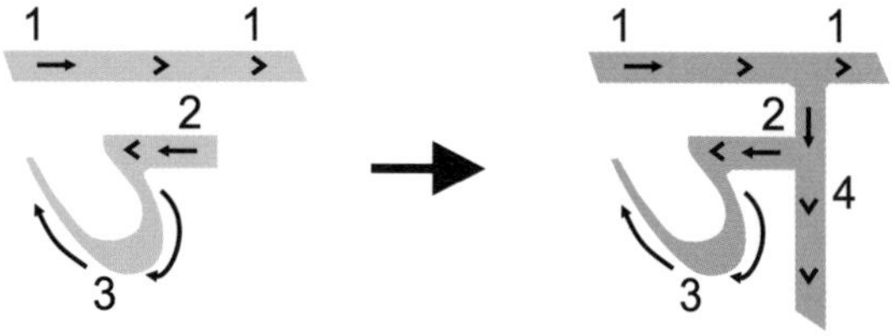

= ज (ja)

ज

ज

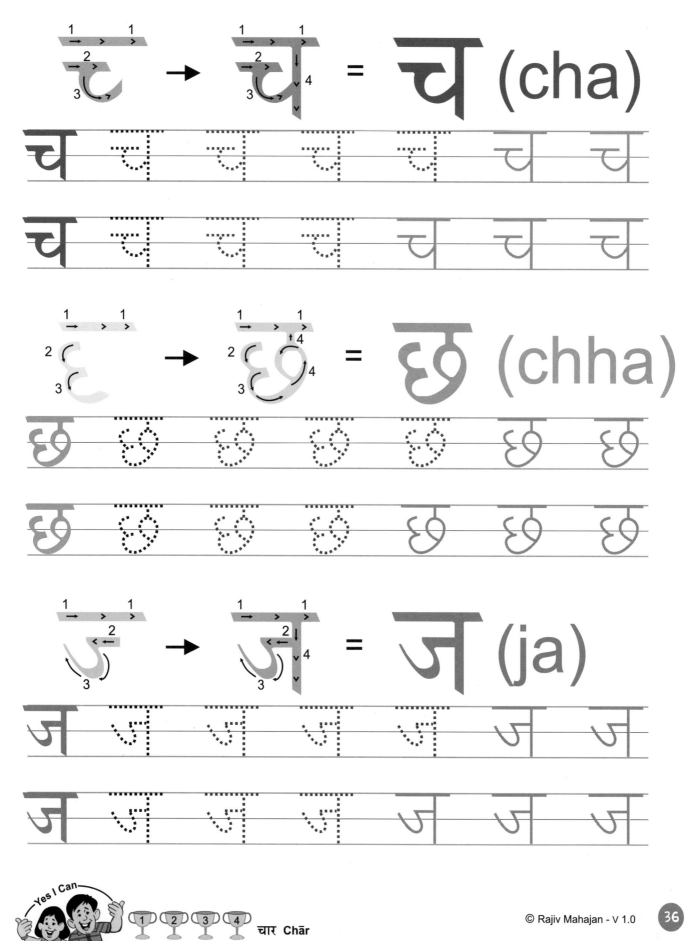

Hindi Word Building

◌ु + च = चु
चु + प = चुप
chu + p = chup (Silence)

म + ◌ू = मू
मू + न = मून
mū + n = mūn (Moon)

◌ु + ब = बु
बु + क = बुक
bu + k = buk (Book)

छ + ◌ा = छा
त + ◌ा = ता
छा + ता = छाता
chhā + tā = chhātā (Umbrella)

ब + ◌ा = बा
ज + ◌ू = जू
बा + जू = बाजू
bā + jū = bājū (Arm)

ज + ◌ी = जी
जी + भ = जीभ
jī + bh = jībh (Tongue)

Build the following words

ची	+	ज	=	______			जू	+	ता	=	______		
ना	+	नी	=	______			चा	+	कू	=	______		
छु	+	प	+	ना	=	______	जू	+	न	=	______		
चु	+	न	+	ना	=	______	भा	+	ग	+	ना	=	______

Combine the letters to form words

Example: chu + p = चुप

chhū	+	nā	=	______			chā	+	kū	=	______		
pū	+	jā	=	______			chū	+	nā	=	______		
chā	+	bī	=	______			kā	+	jū	=	______		
nā	+	ju	+	k	=	______	nū	+	ta	+	n	=	______
ka	+	chhu	+	ā	=	______	ju	+	nū	+	n	=	______

Let's have some fruits!

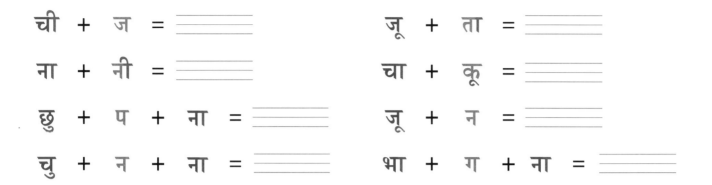

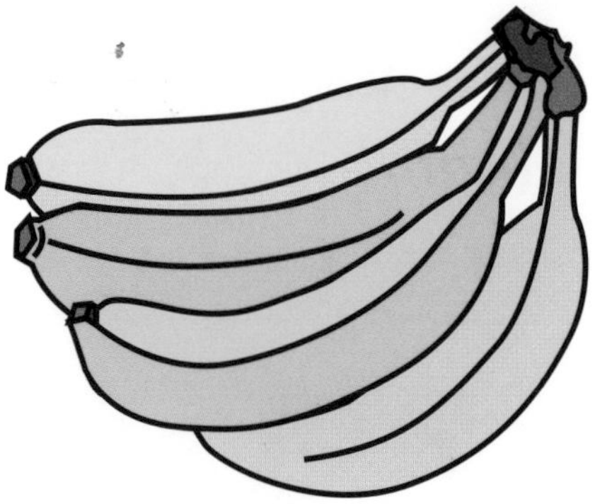

केला **keLā Banana**

Word Meaning

कछुआ → kachhuā
Turtle

चाकू → chākū
Knife

जूता → jūtā → Shoe

चीनी → chīnī
Sugar

चाबी → chābī → Key

चपाती → chapātī
Indian Bread

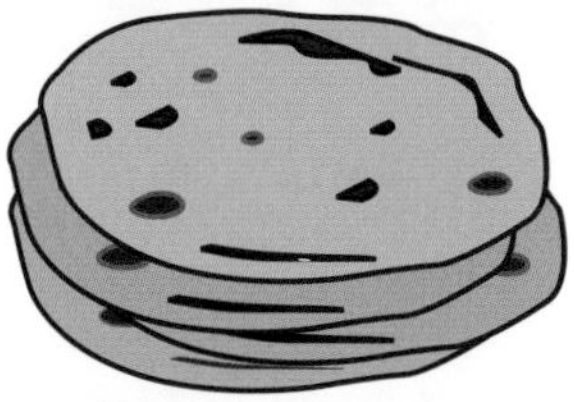

ऊन → ūn → Wool

चीता → chītā
Cheetah

Fill in the blanks

Example: chhu + p = छुप

pū	+	jā		= ____ जा	chā	+	kū		= चा ____
chu	+	n		= ____ न	kā	+	jū		= का ____
chu	+	bh		= ____ भ	ū	+	n		= ____ न
ka	+	chhu	+ ā	= क ____ आ	nū	+	ta	+ n	= ____ तन
nā	+	ju	+ k	= ना ____ क	ju	+	nū	+ n	= ____ नून

Match the following

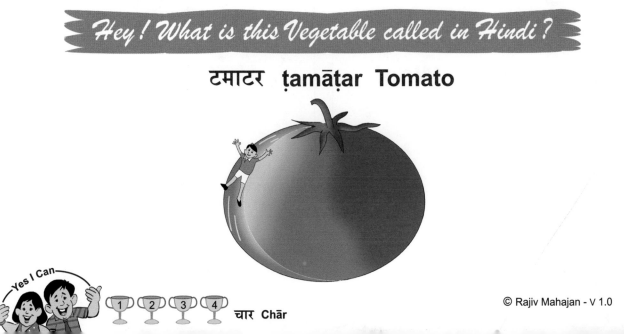

chup	छुप	kājū	चुभ
chhup	चुप	chubh	काजू
jūn	चाकू	chhūnā	पूजा
kachhuā	जून	bājū	छूना
chākū	कछुआ	pūjā	चीनी
jībh	जीभ	chīnī	बाजू

Hey! What is this Vegetable called in Hindi?

टमाटर ṭamāṭar Tomato

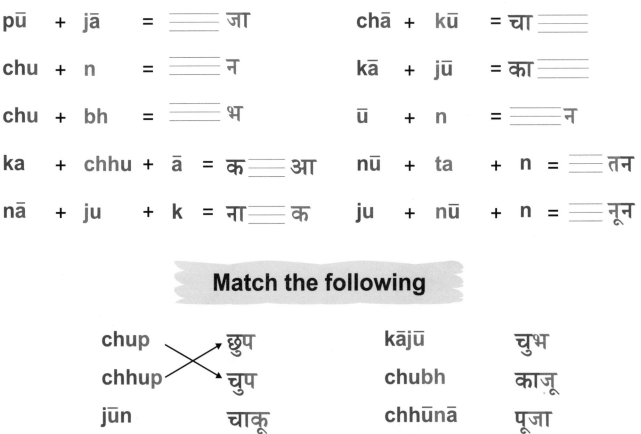

Reading

न	म	ग	ब	व	क	त	भ	प	च	छ	ज
na	ma	ga	ba	va	ka	ta	bha	pa	cha	chha	ja

आ	इ	ई	उ	ऊ
◌ा	ि◌	◌ी	◌ु	◌ू
ā	i	ī	u	ū

पापा, चाचा, छाता, जाना, वाना, ताना, आना

जीन, छीन, बीच, कीच, तीज

चाबी, भाभी, नाभी, कवी, कभी, तभी

बुक, नुक, छुक, चुप, छुप, गुम

भानू, चाचू, बाजू, बानू, नानू, चाकू, काजू

पानी कम पी। गीत गा। भीतर जा।

चीता भाग। भाग मत। चुप चाप भाग जा।

छुप मत। तब तक जीत। छूना मत।

छिप जा। पवन बाजा बजा। चाबी छीन।

मीना नाच। नाक मत छू। छाता छुपा।

पूजा गीत गा। कनक बात बता।

नानी मत जा। कछुआ भागा।

Smooth sailing ! Great !

Now go to page 6-7 and check

LESSON-5

A new language opens new doors !

Letters

र

ख

(ra) run

(kha) khaki

ल

(La) Love

ए ◌े

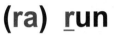

ऐ ◌ै

(e) play

(ai) high

			Vowel	Vowel Sign	Sound Like		
र	ra	run	ए, ऐ	◌े ◌ै	e, ai	रे, रै	re, rai
ख	kha	khaki	ए, ऐ	◌े ◌ै	e, ai	खे, खै	khe, khai
ल	La	Love	ए, ऐ	◌े ◌ै	e, ai	ले, लै	Le, Lai

Letter Writing

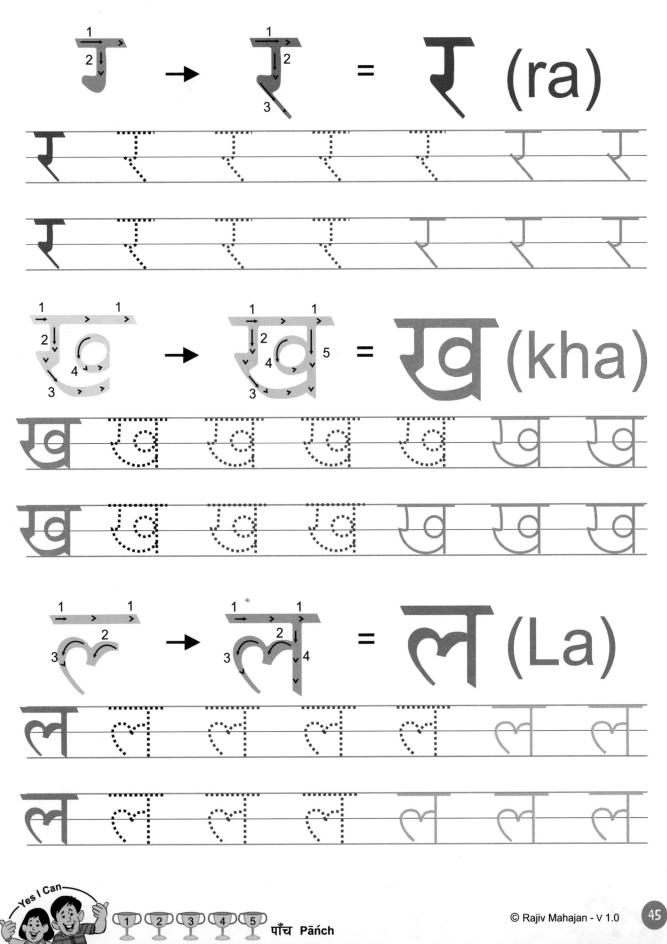

= र (ra)

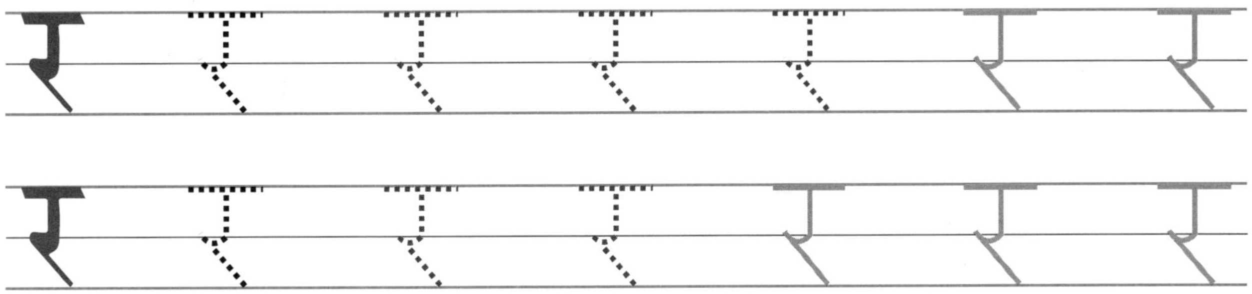

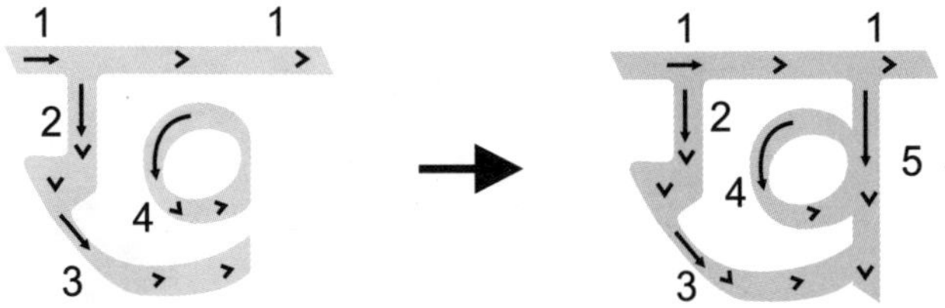

= ख (kha)

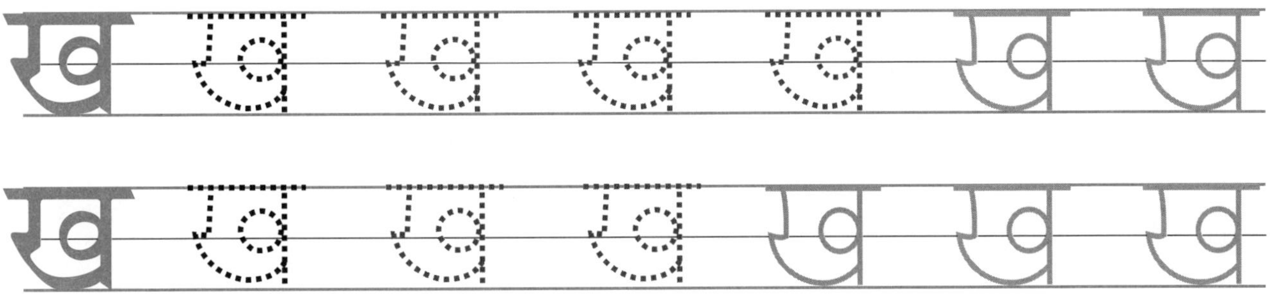

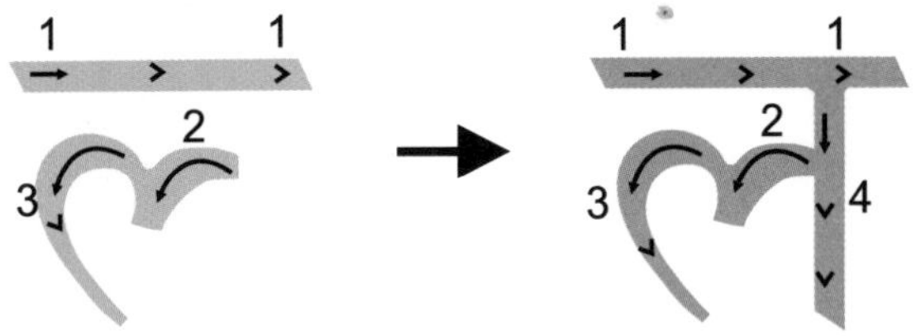

= ल (La)

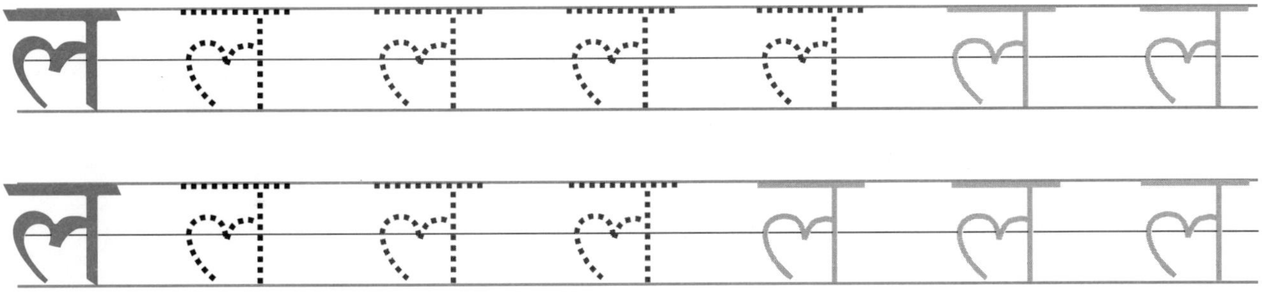

Hindi Word Building

◌े + र = रे

रे + ल = रेल

re + L = reL (Train)

ग + म + ल + ◌े = ले

ग + म + ले = गमले

ga + ma + Le = gamaLe (Flower pots)

ख + ◌े = खे

खे + ल = खेल

khe + L = kheL (Game)

ब + ◌ै = बै

बै + ल = बैल

bai + L = baiL (Ox)

◌े + क = के

के + त + ली = केतली

ke + ta + Lī = ketaLī (Kettle)

त + ◌ै = तै

तै + र + ना = तैरना

tai + ra + nā = tairanā (Swim)

Build the following words

मे + ल = _____

के + क = _____

जे + ल = _____

बे + ल + न = _____

जे + ब = _____

ता + ले = _____

खे + ल + ना = _____

का + ग + ज = _____

Combine the letters to form words

Example: khe + t = खेत

me + Lā = _____

re + t = _____

che + n = _____

je + La + r = _____

ā + Lū = _____

rā + nī = _____

gai + r = _____

mai + Lā = _____

Let's Find the colorful words of Hindi !

हरा   harā   Green

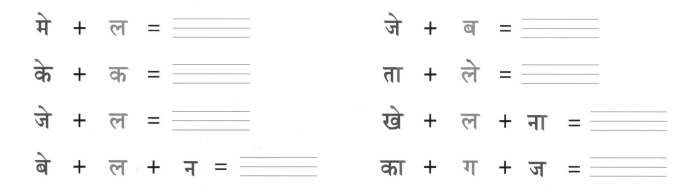

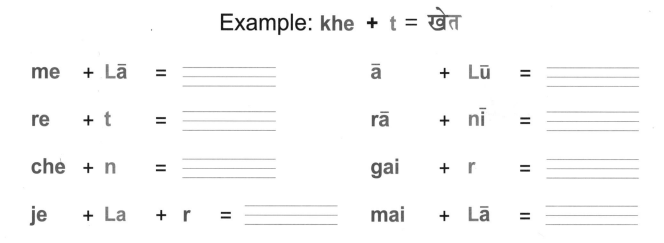

Word Meaning

मेला → meLā → Fair

खेत → khet → Farm

नेता → netā → Leader

मछली → machhaLī
Fish

बतख → batakh → Duck

बेलन → beLan → Roller

कमान → kamān
Bow String

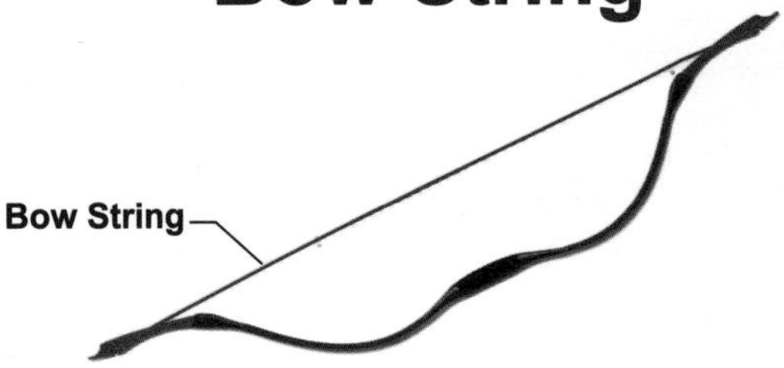

छत → chhat → Roof

Fill in the blanks

Example: khe + L = खेल

re	+ n	=	____न		jai	+ m	=	____म
mai	+ p	=	____प		re	+ L	=	____ल
me	+ L	=	____ल		je	+ L	=	____ल
je	+ La + r	=	____लर		ke	+ va + L	=	____वल
vai	+ n	=	____न		khe	+ La + nā	=	____लना

Match the following

jaim	जेल	pāgaL	रेन
jeL	जैम	ren	पागल
ret	कलम	kheLanā	केवल
kaLam	रेत	kevaL	तैरना
chhat	नेपाल	reL	खेलना
nepāL	छत	tairanā	रेल

Taste some fruits!

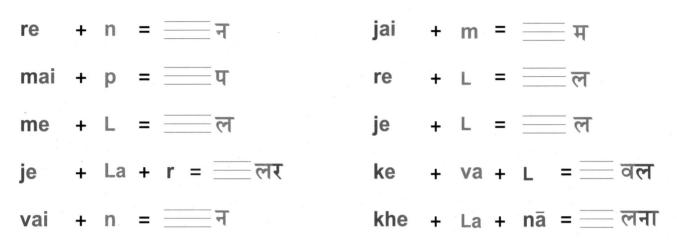

अंगूर aṅgūr Grapes

Reading

न	म	ग	ब	व	क	त	भ	प	च	छ	ज	र	ख	ल
na	ma	ga	ba	va	ka	ta	bha	pa	cha	chha	ja	ra	kha	La

आ	इ	ई	उ	ऊ	ए	ऐ
ा	ि	ी	ु	ू	े	ै
ā	i	ī	u	ū	e	ai

बाल, जाल, खाल, माल, ताल, गाल

कागज, चावल, पागल, काजल, मानव

जिगर, रिबन, चिराग, विराग

जीवन, बीमा, पीला, नीला, चीला, तीला

गुलाल, गुलाब, गुलाबी, बुखार, भूचाल, कुनाल

पूरी, जूरी, जूता, चूना, लुभाना, जुबान

रेल, तेल, खेल, चेला, मेला, बेला

मैला, गैर, बैर, खैर, तैर

बेकार, जेलर, तेवर, जेवर, लेबर

रेल तेज चली। गीता किताब लिख। खत लिख।

लेखक किताब लिखेगा। कागज की नाव बना।

मेले में जा। मेले में खेल। केला खा। गेम मत खेल।

गमले छत पर रख। जग में पानी लेजा।

कवि कविता लिख। माता पिता के चरन छू। बैर मत कर।

मैला मत कर। बाजार चल। जेब खाली कर।

I can easily twist a tale or two now !

Go check on page 6-7

LESSON-6

We are entering an amazing new world !

Letters

स

श

(sa) sun

(sha) shell

फ

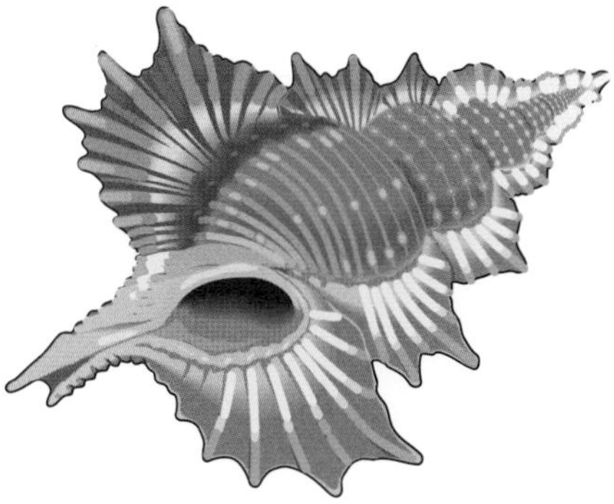

(pha, fa) fan

ओ ◌ो

औ ◌ौ

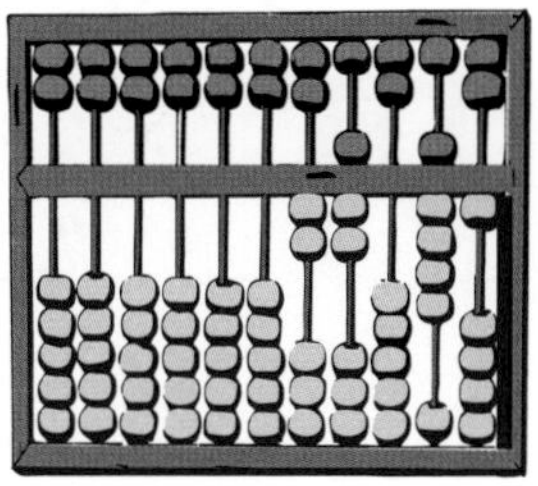

(o) go

(ou) count

			Vowel	Vowel Sign	Sound Like		
स	sa	sun	ओ, औ	◌ो ◌ौ	o, au	सो, सौ	so, sau
श	sha	shell	ओ, औ	◌ो ◌ौ	o, au	शो, शौ	sho, shau
फ	pha	fan	ओ, औ	◌ो ◌ौ	o, au	फो, फौ	fo, fau

Letter Writing

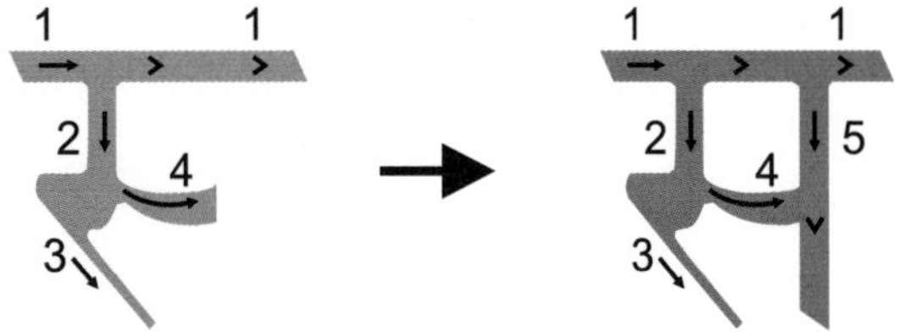

= स (sa)

स स स स स स स

स स स स स स स

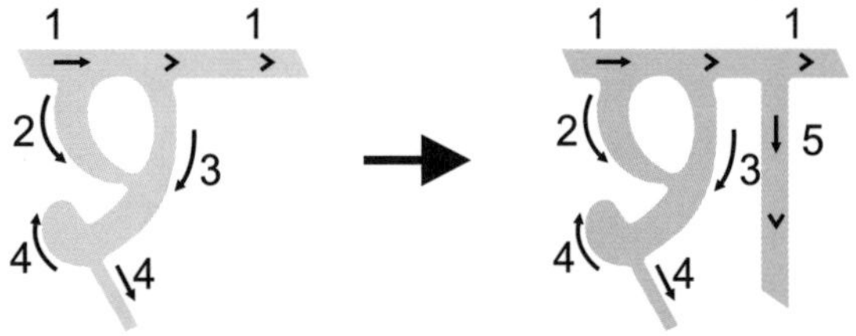

= श (sha)

श श श श श श श

श श श श श श श

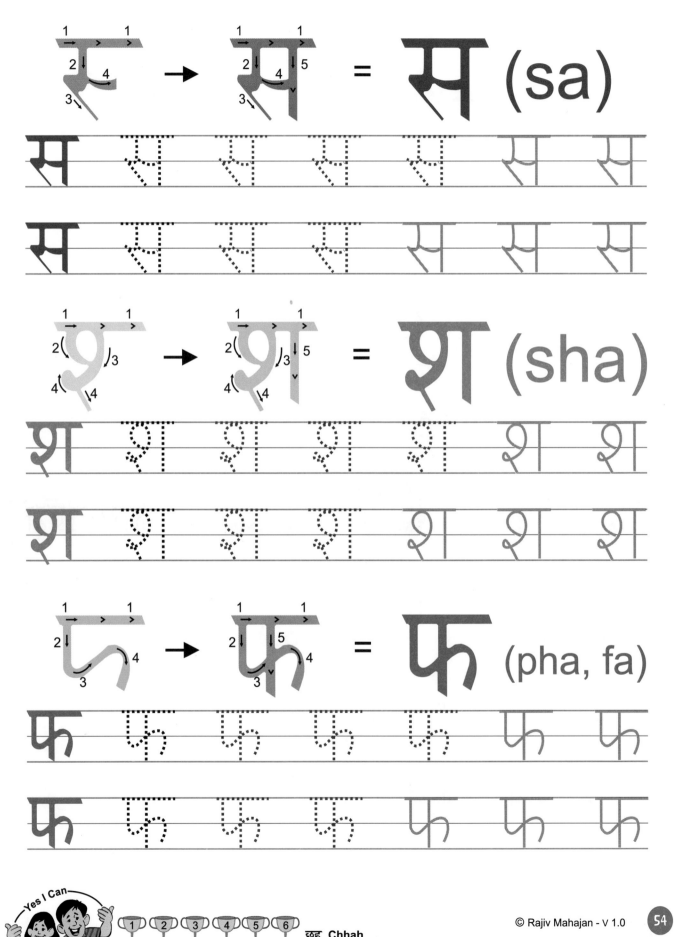

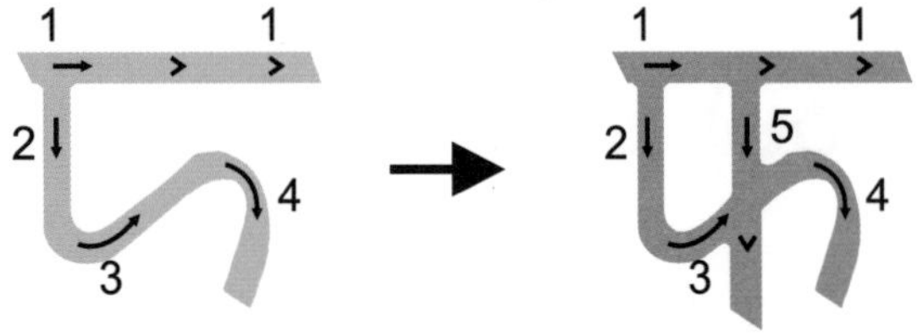

= फ (pha, fa)

फ फ फ फ फ फ फ

फ फ फ फ फ फ फ

Hindi Word Building

त + ◌ो = तो

त + ◌ा = ता

तो + ता = तोता

to + tā = totā **(Parrot)**

म + ◌ो = मो

मो + र = मोर

mo + r = mor **(Peacock)**

फ + ◌ौ = फौ

ज + ◌ी = जी

फौ + जी = फौजी

fau + jī = faujī **(Soldier)**

स + ◌ौ = सौ

sa + au = sau **(Hundred)**

फ + ◌ो = फो

फो + न = फोन

pho + n = phon **(Phone)**

ख + ◌ि = खि

ल + ◌ौ = लौ

न + ◌ा = ना

खि + लौ + ना = खिलौना

khi + Lau + nā = khiLaunā **(Toy)**

Build the following words

सो + ना =

फू + ल =

मे + ज =

रो + ना =

सा + बु + न =

कौ + आ =

गो + ल =

बो + ल + ना =

औ + र + त =

गि + ला + स =

Combine the letters to form words

Example: kho + j = खोज

bhā + Lū =

sho + r =

pai + r =

ba + ka + rī =

mo + ra + nī =

pau + nā =

shau + k =

bā + ri + sh =

nau + ka + r =

sū + ra + j =

Let's go green with vegetables!

पालक pāLak Spinach

Word Meaning

साबुन → sābun → Soap

फूल → fūL → Flower

सूरज → sūraj → Sun

भालू → bhāLū → Bear

औरत → aurat → Lady

बकरी → bakarī → Goat

मेज → mej → Table

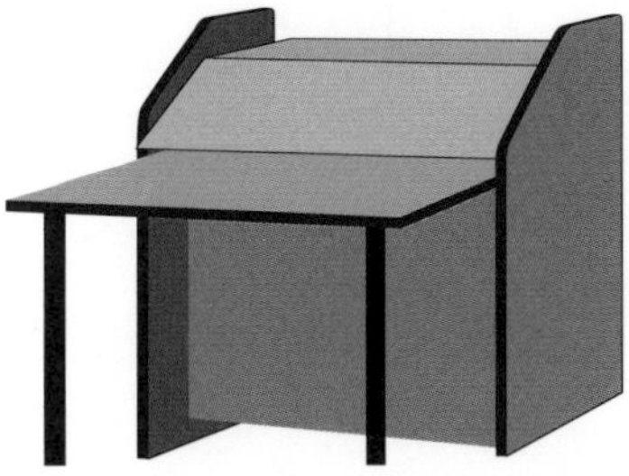

नाखून → nākhūn
Nail

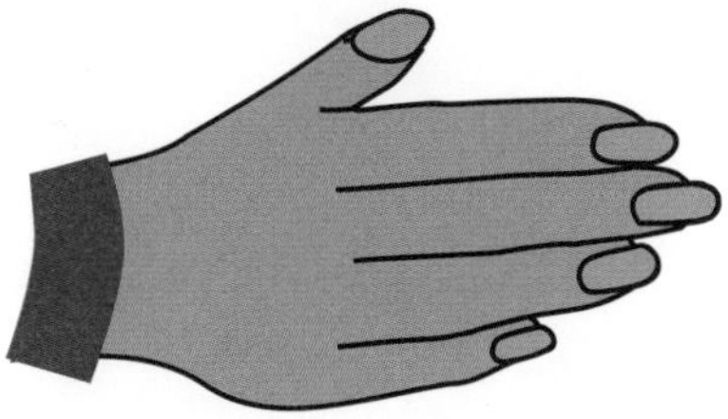

Fill in the blanks

Example: bo + L = बोल

so	+	nā	=	____ना	kho	+	j	= ____ज
cho	+	r	=	____र	fū	+	L	= ____ल
mo	+	r	=	____र	go	+	L	= ____ल
kā	+	nū	+ n	= का____न	bo	+ La	+ nā	= ____लना
po	+	shā	+ k	= ____शाक	Li	+ kha	+ nā	= ____खना

Match the following

chor	कौआ	mej	फूल
kauā	चोर	sonā	मेज
poshāk	बोलना	fūL	सोना
moranī	खिलौना	aurat	गिलास
boLanā	पोशाक	giLās	खोजना
khiLaunā	मोरनी	khojanā	औरत

Let's splash a bit of color!

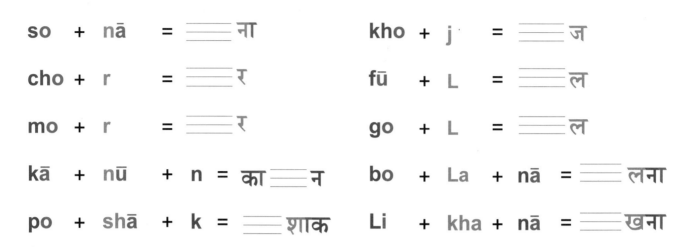

पीला pīLā Yellow

Reading

न	म	ग	ब	व	क	त	भ	प	च	छ	ज	र	ख	ल
na	ma	ga	ba	va	ka	ta	bha	pa	cha	chha	ja	ra	kha	La

आ	इ	ई	उ	ऊ	ए	ऐ	ओ	औ
ा	ि	ी	ु	ू	े	ै	ो	ौ
ā	i	ī	u	ū	e	ai	o	au

सिर, गिर, फिर, किन, लिख, सिक

शिमला, सिगार, फिराक, किताब, खिलाफ, जिराफ

सेफ, शैफ, पैर, खैर सूप, फूल, जून

गोल, बोल, तोल, पोल, खोल, शोर, मोर, जोर

फौरन, सौरभ, गौरव, शौक, वौकर, नौकर

शोर मत कर। सेब खा। बारिश मे मत भीग। शूरवीर बन।

पुजारी पूजा कर। छत पर मत सो। सौ तक गिन।

गोल गोल भाग। फूल मत फेक। रो मत, खिलौने से खेल।

ताजे फल खा। शौक से फल खा। नौकरी पर जा।

शिकारी शिकार कर। शिमला चल। खरगोश भागा।

फोन कर। फूल मत फेंक। फौजी फौज में जा।

पानी का गिलास भर। बकरी घास खाएगी।

छत से चोर भागा। पुलिस पीछे भागी।

जोर से बोल। पोल मत खोल। भगवान की पूजा कर।

So fascinating ! So different !

Go check on page 6-7

LESSON-7

Jump into the pool !

Letters

ट

(ṭa) cuṭ

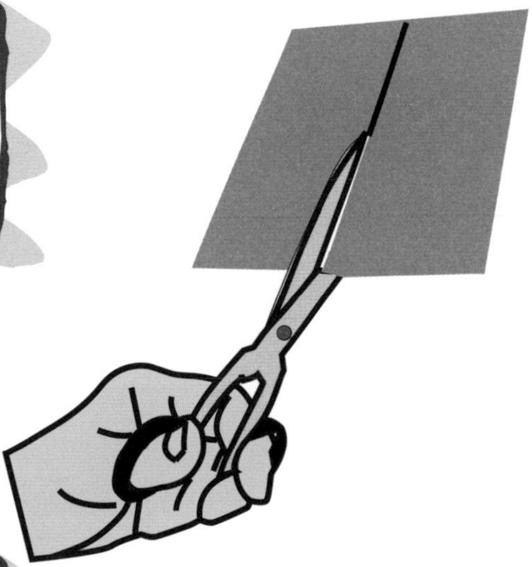

य

(ya) yes

ह

(ha) hug

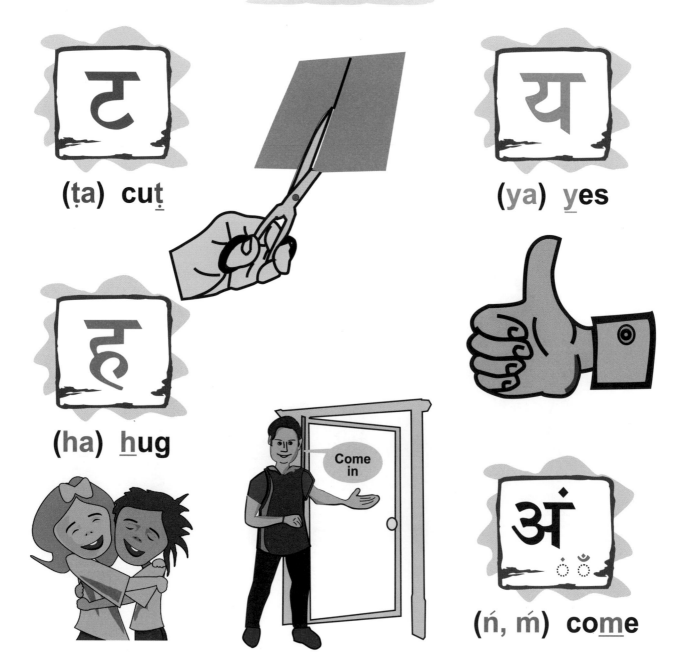

अं

ं ँ

(ń, ḿ) come

			Vowel	Vowel Sign	Sound Like	
ट	ṭa	cuṭ	अं	ं ँ	ń, ḿ	टं, टँ
य	ya	yes	अं	ं ँ	ń, ḿ	यं, यँ
ह	ha	hug	अं	ं ँ	ń, ḿ	हं, हँ

Letter Writing

= ट (ṭa)

ट ट ट ट ट ट ट

ट ट ट ट ट ट ट

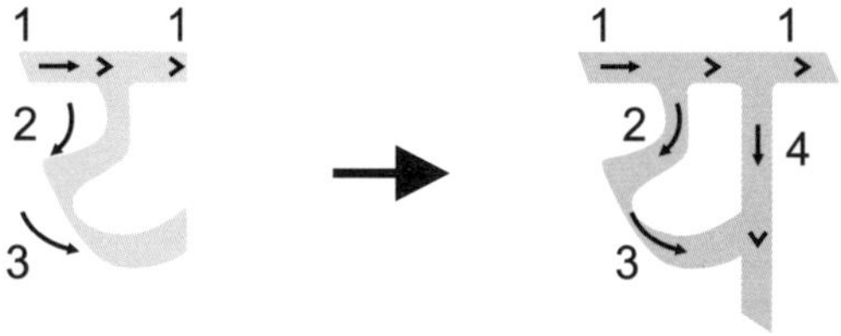

= य (ya)

य य य य य य य

य य य य य य य

= ह (ha)

ह ह ह ह ह ह ह

ह ह ह ह ह ह ह

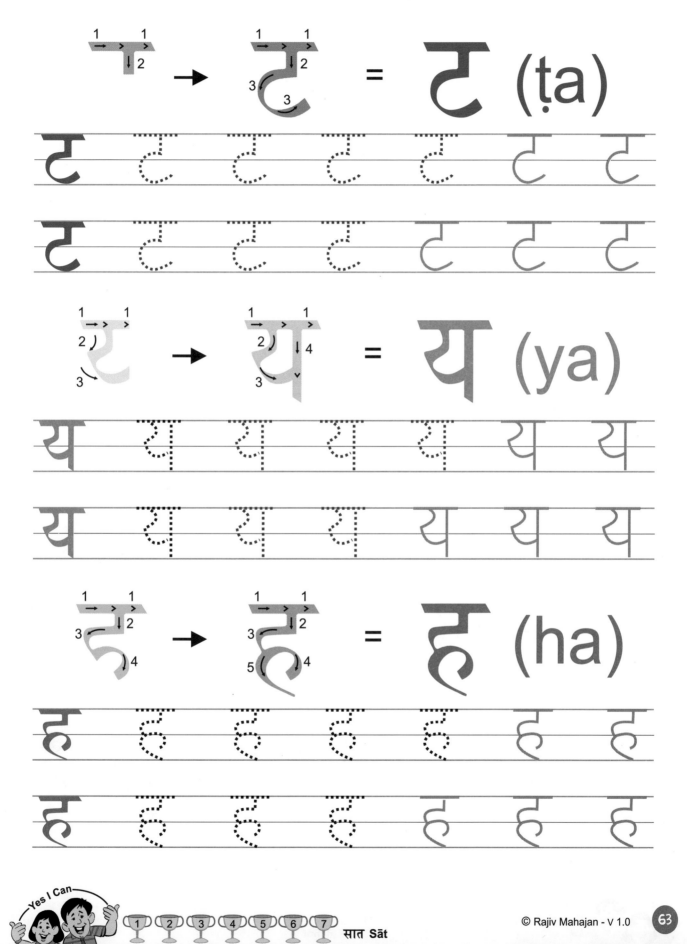

Hindi Word Building

र + ◌ं = रं
रं + ग = रंग
rań + g = rańg (color)

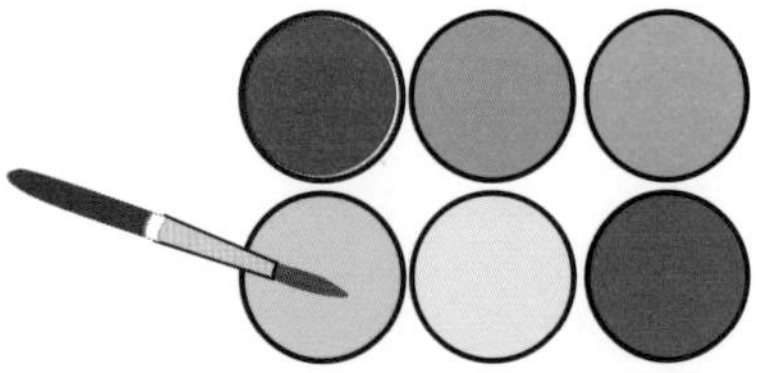

आ + ◌ँ = आँ
आँ + ख = आँख
āń + kh = āńkh (Eye)

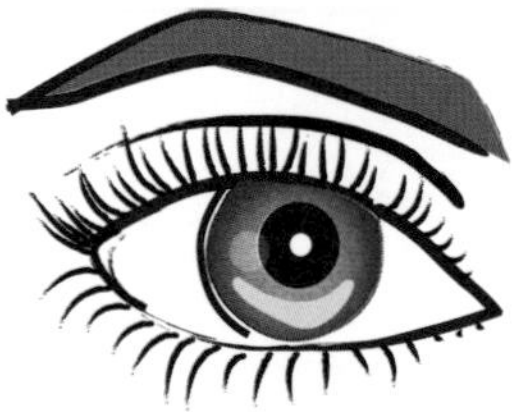

पा + ◌ँ = पाँ
पाँ + च = पाँच
pāń + ch = pāńch (Five)

प + त + ◌ं = पतं
प + तं + ग = पतंग
pa + tań + g = patańg (Kite)

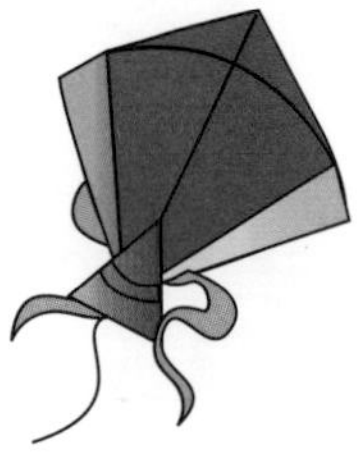

ह + ◌ँ = हँ
हँ + स = हँस
न + ◌ा = ना
हँ + स + ना = हँसना
hań + sa + nā = hańsanā (Smile)

बा + ◌ँ = बाँ
स + ◌ु = सु
र + ◌ी = री
बाँ + सु + री = बाँसुरी
bāń + su + rī = bāńsurī (Flute)

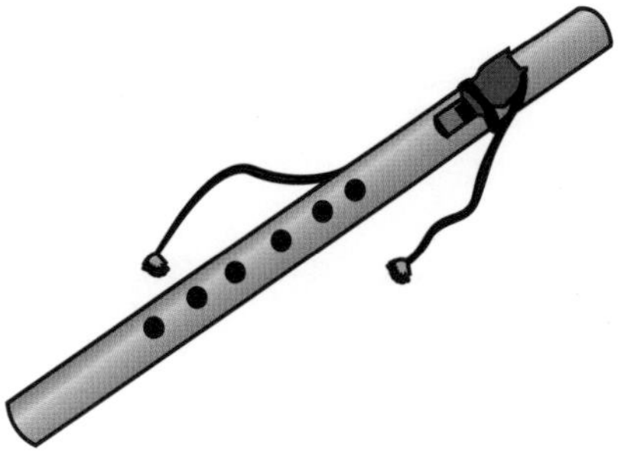

Build the following words

गाँ + व = ______ तॉँ + गा = ______

य + हाँ = ______ पं + ख = ______

व + हाँ = ______ शं + ख = ______

हाँ + फ + ना = ______ इ + जं + न = ______

काँ + प + ना = ______ खाँ + स + ना = ______

Combine the letters to form words

Example: **pań** + **kh** = पँख

ja + ńg = ______ fań + sī = ______

hī + rā = ______ ka + ṭo + rī = ______

khī + rā = ______ ṭo + ka + rī = ______

ti + ta + Lī = ______ fań + sa + nā = ______

ta + ra + ńg = ______ jań + ga + L = ______

Let's go green with vegetables!

प्याज pyāj Onion

Word Meaning

पँखा → pańkhā → Fan

तिरंगा → tirańgā
Indian Flag

तितलियाँ → titaLiyāń
Butterflies

उंगलियाँ → uńgaLiyāń
Fingers

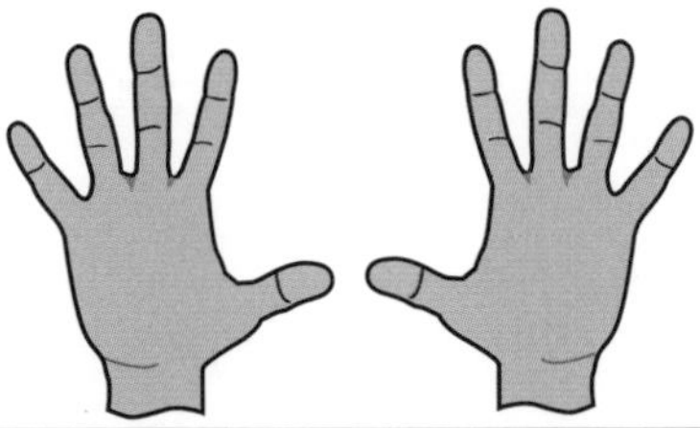

अंगूर → ańgūr
Grapes

चूहा → chūhā → Rat

पंख → pańkh → Wing

चेहरा → cheharā → Face

Fill in the blanks

Example: ba + hu + t = बहुत

ṭo	+ pī		= टो____	tā	+ Lā		= ता____
chū	+ hā		= ____हा	khi	+ Lau	+ nā	= खि____ना
tau	+ Li	+ yā	= तौलि____	bi	+ ja	+ Lī	= बिज____
ti	+ ta	+ Lī	= ____तली	ta	+ rā	+ jū	= तरा____
bo	+ ta	+ L	= ____तल	ṭ	+ ha	+ nī	= ट____

Match the following

mayūr	जंग	bahut	रंग
jańg	मयूर	tirańgā	बहुत
tāLā	बुक	rańg	तितली
buk	ताला	ṭopī	तिरंगा
bīmār	युवक	titaLī	टोपी
yuvak	बीमार		

Let's have some fruits!

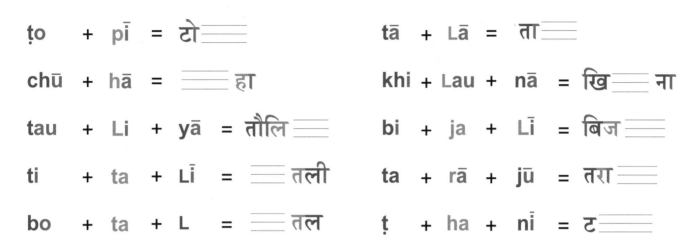

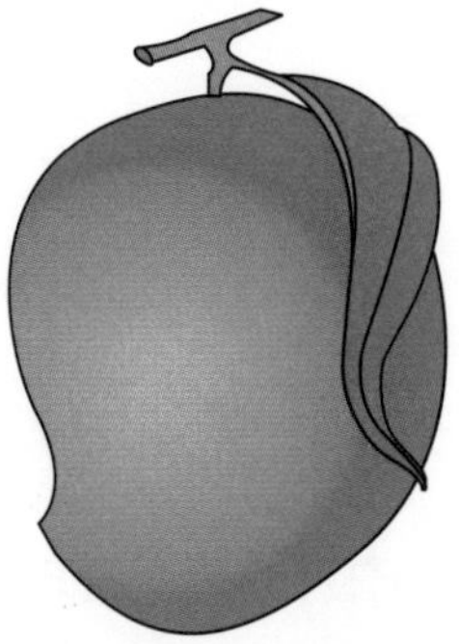

आम ām Mango

Reading

न	म	ग	ब	व	क	त	भ	प	च	छ
na	ma	ga	ba	va	ka	ta	bha	pa	cha	chha

ज	र	ख	ल	स	श	फ	ट	य	ह
ja	ra	kha	La	sa	sha	pha, fa	ṭa	ya	ha

आ	इ	ई	उ	ऊ	ए	ऐ	ओ	औ	अं
◌ा	◌ि	◌ी	◌ु	◌ू	◌े	◌ै	◌ो	◌ौ	◌ं ◌ँ
ā	i	ī	u	ū	e	ai	o	au	ń, ḿ

कंगन, आंगन, जंगल, तरंग, पलंग, पतंग

रंग, यंग, भंग, जंग, तंग,

चूहा, टोपी, युवक, गोली, टेप, चेप, टैरो

हौरन, हैरान, हैवान, टैरन, हिसाब

किरन, हिरन, टिफिन, टिकट, सिमट

उसकी कार लाल रंग की है। मोर की आँख का रंग नीला है।

खरगोश तेज भागता है। मोहन बाँसूरी बजाता है।

भालू नाचता है। मोर बारिश में नाचता है।

शेर जंगल मे रहता है। पँखा बिजली से चलता है।

खरगोश सफेद रंग का होता है। वह सो रहा है।

वह कभी – कभी टोपी पहनता है।

मैं काम करना चाहता हूँ। वह पैसा चाहता है।

तिरंगा तीन रंग का होता है। चूहा काले रंग का है।

सभी मिलजुल कर आंगन में खेलते है।

It's so cool !

Go on and check on page 6-7

LESSON-8

Focus man !
Target one at a time !

Letters

घ

(gha) ghost

द

(da) other
(Close to father)

ध

(dha) buddha

थ

(tha) thunder

घ	gha	ghost
द	da	other
ध	dha	buddha
थ	tha	thunder

Letter Writing

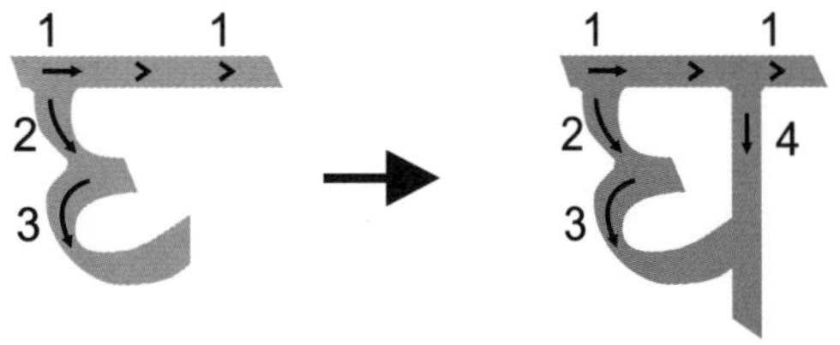

= घ (gha)

घ

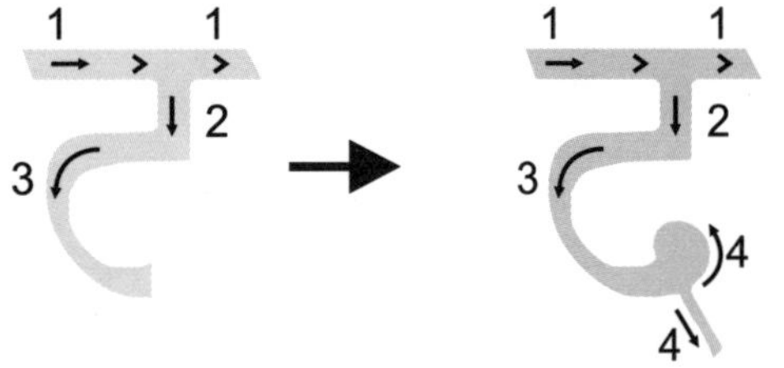

= द (da)

द

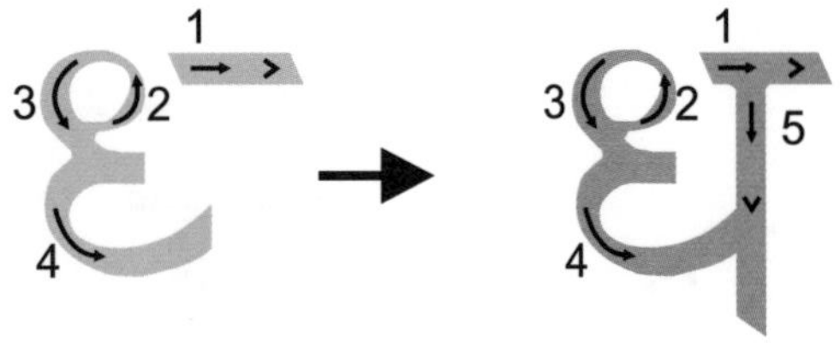

= ध (dha)

ध

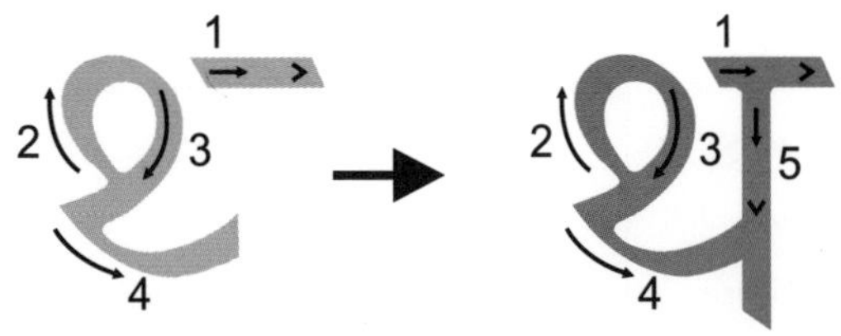

= थ (tha)

थ

Hindi Word Building

द + ◌ी = दी

व + ◌ा = वा

दी + वा + र = दीवार

dī + wā + r = dīwār (wall)

ह + ◌ा = हा

थ + ◌ी = थी

हा + थी = हाथी

hā + thī = hāthī (Elephant)

ध + ◌ो = धो

ब + ◌ी = बी

धो + बी = धोबी

dho + bī = dhobī (Laundryman)

ब + ◌ं = बं

बं + द = बंद

बं + द + र = बंदर

bań + da + r = bańdar (Monkey)

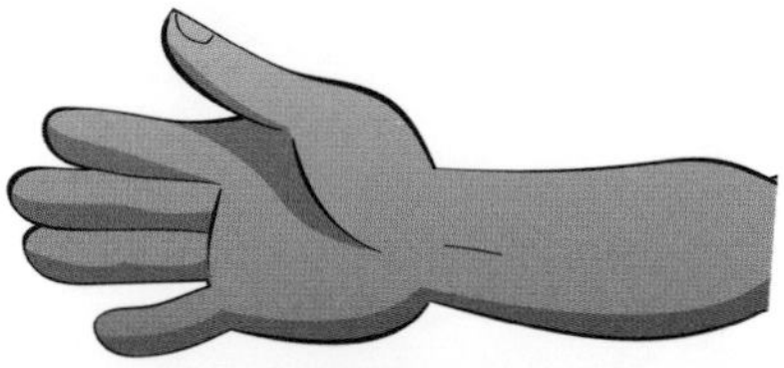

ह + ◌ा = हा

हा + थ = हाथ

hā + th = hāth (Hand)

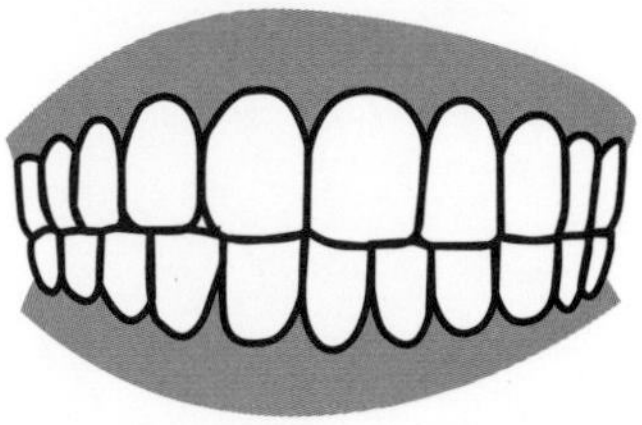

द + ◌ा + ◌ं = दां

दां + त = दांत

dāń + t = dāńt (Teeth)

Build the following words

थै + ला = ______ जा + दू = ______

धा + गा = ______ पौ + धा = ______

ले + ख + क = ______ क + हा + नी = ______

घु + ट + ना = ______ भू + ल + ना = ______

दे + ख + ना = ______ कू + द + ना = ______

Combine the letters to form words

Example: du + kh = दुख

dhū + p = ______ dā + dī = ______

dū + dh = ______ di + yā = ______

gha + r = ______ khī + rā = ______

pu + dī + nā = ______ dha + ra + tī = ______

ga + ra + mī = ______ pu + jā + rī = ______

Let's hunt for colors in Hindi!

संतरी santarī Orange

Word Meaning

घुटना → ghuṭanā → knee

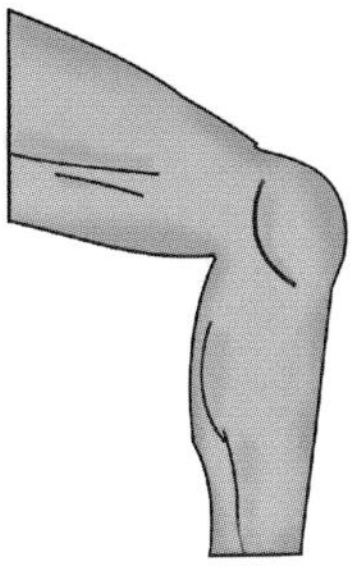

जादू → jādū → Magic

कूदना → kūdanā
Jump

धागा → dhāgā
Thread

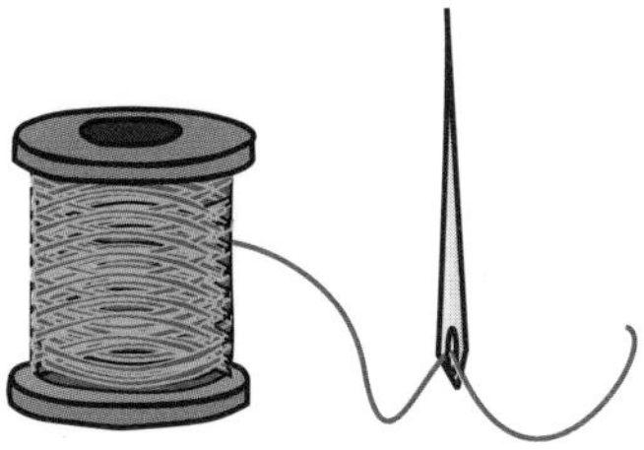

दीपक → dīpak → Lamp

नींबू → nīḿbū
Lemon

गुलाब → guLāb
Rose

थैला → thaiLā
Bag

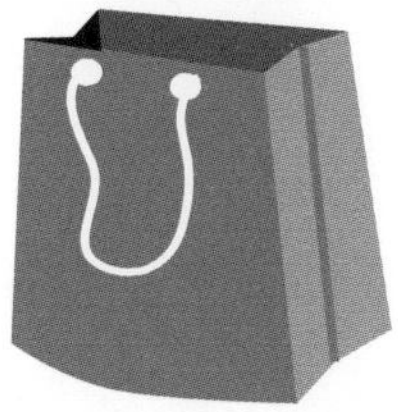

Fill in the blanks

Example: dhū + p = धूप

jā	+ p		= जा___		ro	+ p		= ___प
du	+ kh		= ___ख		thā	+ Lī		= था___
dha	+ n		= ध___		dhā	+ gā		= ___गा
ghū	+ ma	+ nā	= ___मना		dī	+ wā	+ r	= ___वार
dha	+ ra	+ tī	= धर___		du	+ kā	+ n	= ___कान

Match the following

dūdh	दुख	dīpak	घर
dukh	दूध	dukān	दीपक
thāLī	माली	ghar	धागा
māLī	दीया	dhāgā	दुकान
dīwār	थाली	dādī	घूमना
dīyā	दीवार	ghūmanā	दादी

Hey! Vegetable what's your name?

गोभी gobhī Cauliflower

Reading

न	म	ग	ब	व	क	त	भ	प	च	छ	ज	र
na	ma	ga	ba	va	ka	ta	bha	pa	cha	chha	ja	ra

ख	ल	स	श	फ	ट	य	ह	घ	द	थ	ध
kha	La	sa	sha	pha, fa	ṭa	ya	ha	gha	da	tha	dha

आ	इ	ई	उ	ऊ	ए	ऐ	ओ	औ	अं
◌ा	◌ि	◌ी	◌ु	◌ू	◌े	◌ै	◌ो	◌ौ	◌ं ◌ँ
ā	i	ī	u	ū	e	ai	o	au	ń, ḿ

घर, भर, चर, धर दम, धन, घन, थन

दादी, थाली, ताली, खाली, जाली, माली

दुकान, गुलाब, तुफान, चुनाव, नुकसान, पुराना

धूप, खूब, देना, लेना, दो, खो, धो, खोना, धोना

घेवर, देवर, लैदर, चैनल, बेलन, टेबल

नोट, बोट, वोट, दोनो, बंदर, चंदन, लंदन, बंधन

बंदर वाला आया । बंदर को लाया । बंदर काले रंग का था ।

उसने बंदर का खेल दिखाया । बंदर नाच रहा था ।

बंदर ने केला खाया । सबको बहुत आनंद आया ।

सबने मिलकर ताली बजाई ।

टोकरी में फल रख । हमें ताजे फल खाने चहिए ।

हमें हाथ धोकर खाना खाना चाहिए ।

दादी हमें कहानी सुनाती है । हम अपने माता–पिता का आदर करते हैं ।

वह धीरे–धीरे लिखता है ।

It's so enjoyable !

Now go to page 6-7 and check

LESSON-9

Simple steps make it quick and fast !

Letters

ठ

(ṭha) ṭhug

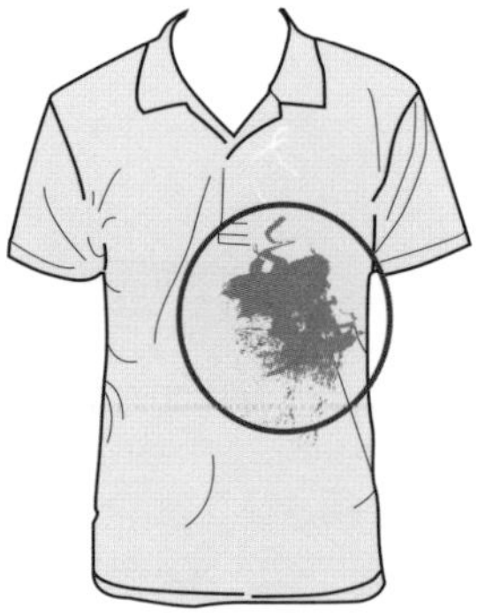

ड

(ḍa) ḍirṭ

Adhere to traffic rules

झ

(jha, za) dodge

ढ

(ḍha) aḍhere

ठ	ṭha	huṭh
ड	ḍa	ḍirṭ
ढ	ḍha	aḍhere
झ	jha, za	dodge

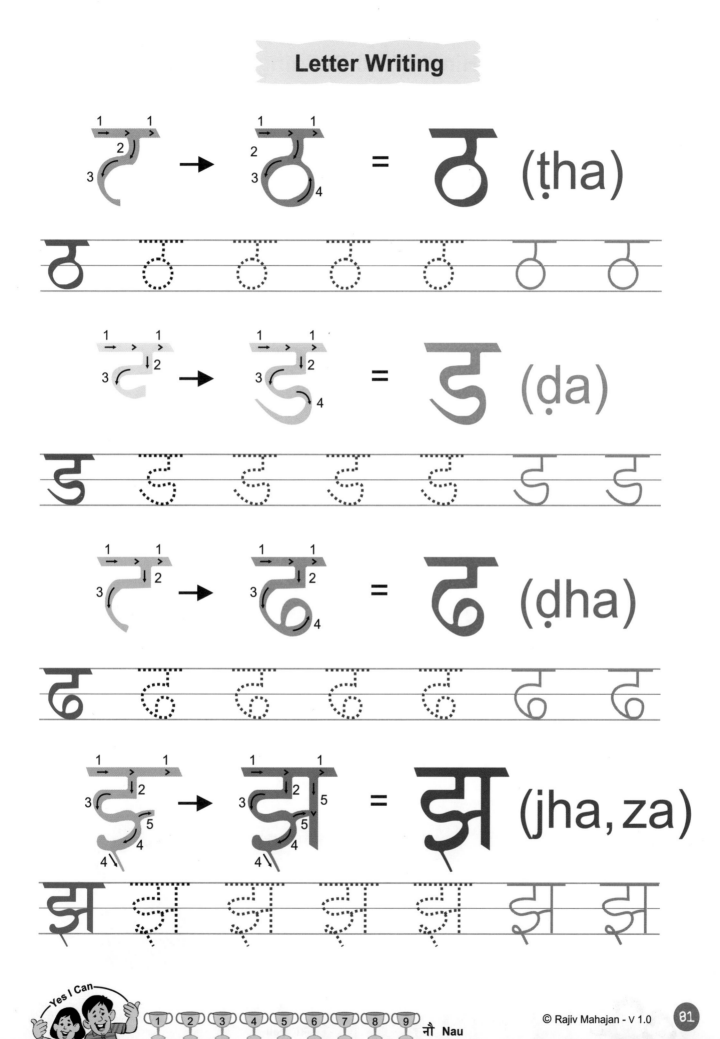

Letter Writing

= ठ (ṭha)

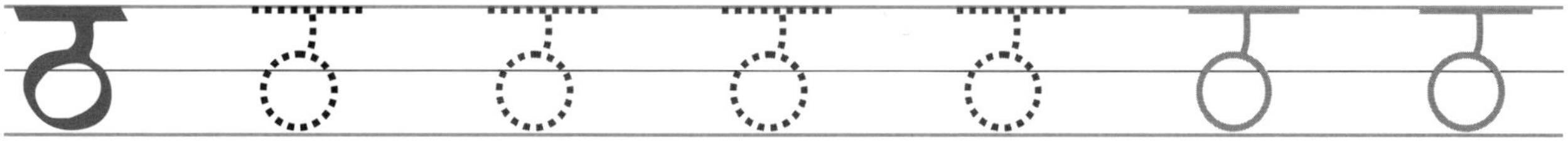

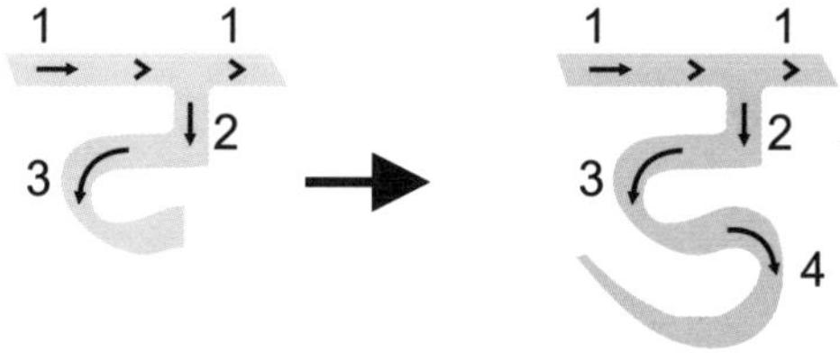

= ड (ḍa)

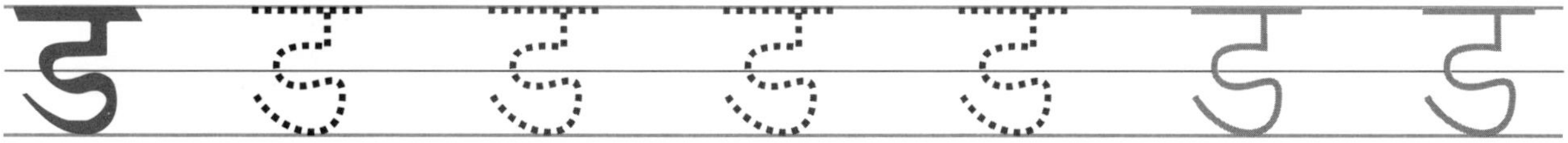

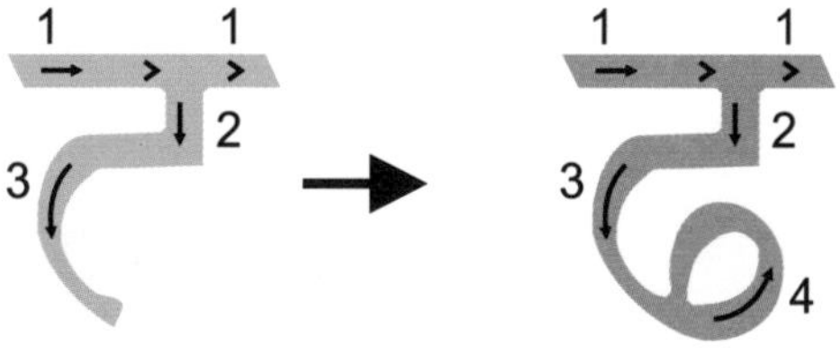

= ढ (ḍha)

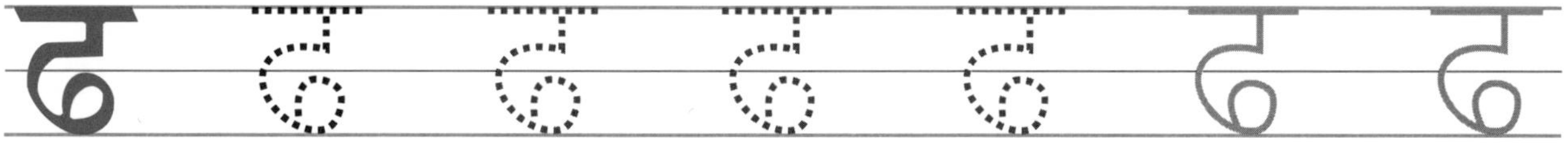

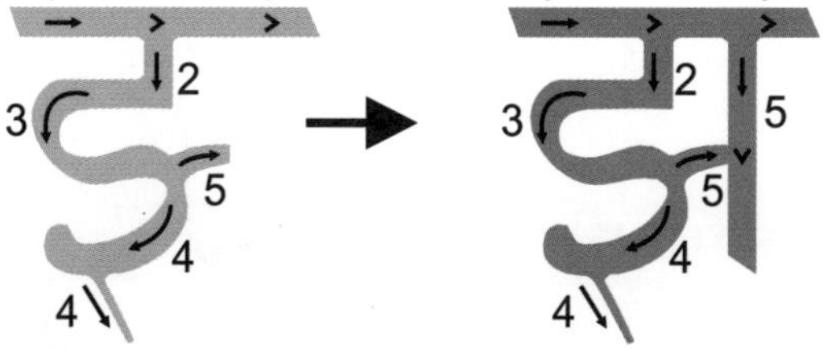

= झ (jha, za)

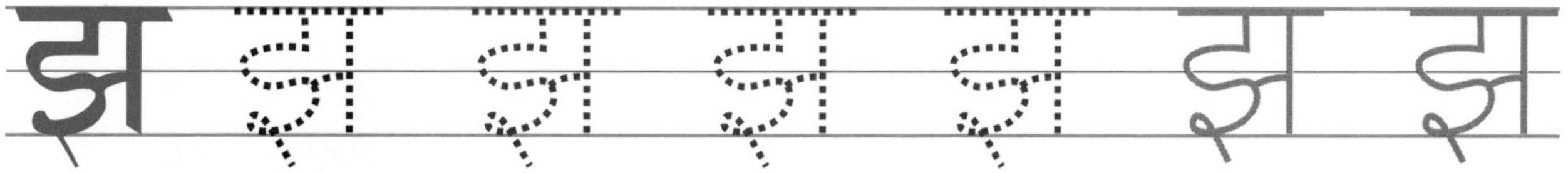

नौ **Nau**

Hindi Word Building

झ + ◌ं = झं
ड + ◌ा = डा
झं + डा = झंडा
jhań + ḍā = jhańḍā **(Flag)**

झ + र = झर
न + ◌ा = ना
झ + र + ना = झरना
jha + ra + nā = jharanā **(Water fall)**

ि◌ + भ + ◌ं = भिं
ड + ◌ी = डी
भिं + डी = भिंडी
bhiń + ḍī = bhińḍī **(Okra)**

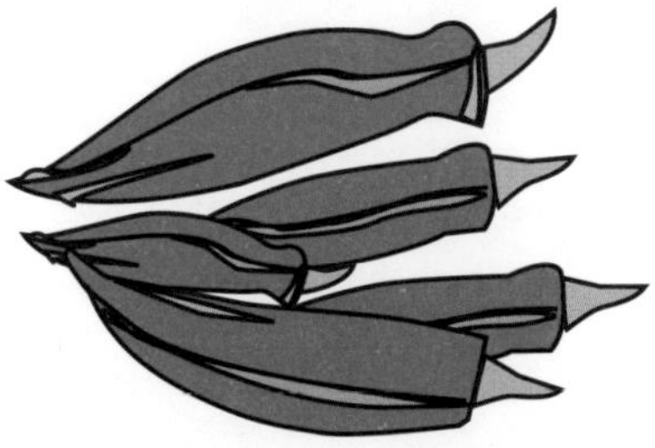

अ + ◌ं = अं
ड + ◌ा = डा
अं + डा = अंडा
ań + ḍā = ańḍā **(Egg)**

ड + ◌ा = डा
ि◌ + क = कि
य + ◌ा = या
डा + कि + या = डाकिया
ḍā + ki + yā = ḍākiyā **(Postman)**

ढ + ◌ो = ढो
ढो + ल = ढोल
ḍho + L = ḍhoL **(Drum)**

Build the following words

ता + रा = ______

शा + खा = ______

ड + र + ना = ______

बै + ठ + ना = ______

मि + ठा + ई = ______

रा + त = ______

ठे + ला = ______

ढ + क + ना = ______

ढ + प + ली = ______

क + हा + नी = ______

Combine the letters to form words

ExampLe: ṭha + g = ठग

rā + jā = ______

kho + nā = ______

pī + sa + nā = ______

Li + fā + fā = ______

su + na + nā = ______

de + nā = ______

Le + nā = ______

pu + dī + nā = ______

bhū + La + nā = ______

ḍū + ba + nā = ______

Want to try some juicy stuff?

झर्भरि jharbhari Strawberry

Word Meaning

गाजर → gājar → Carrot

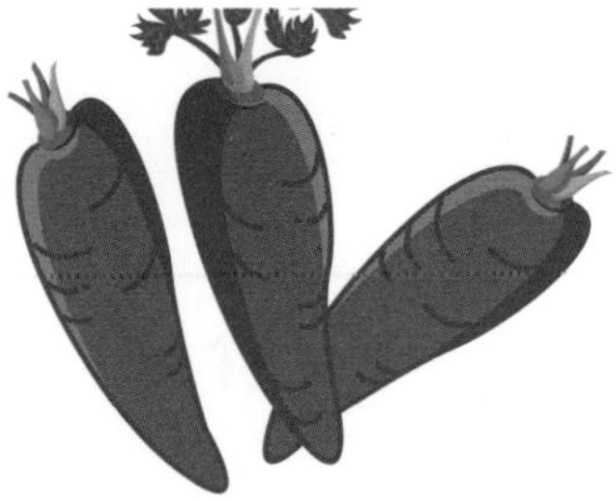

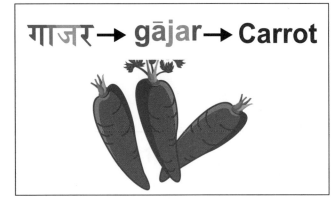

गेंद → geńd → Ball

डाक घर → ḍāk ghar
Post Office

चटाई → chaṭāī → Mat

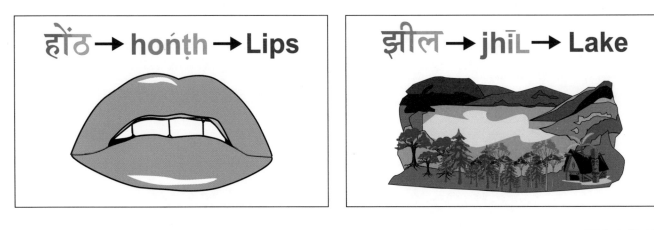

होंठ → hońṭh → Lips

झील → jhīL → Lake

ढाल → ḍhāL → Shield

मिठाई → miṭhāī
Sweet

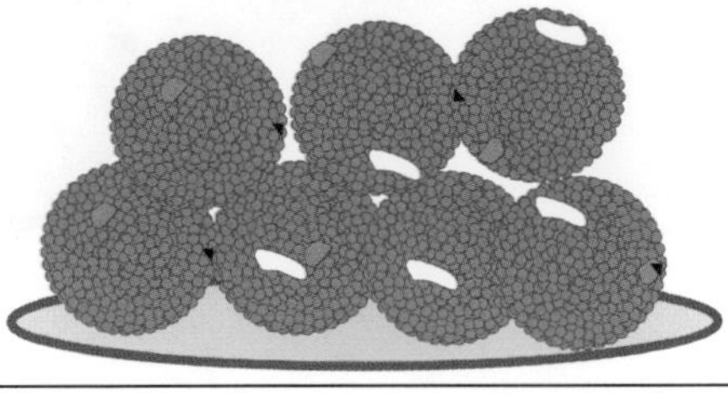

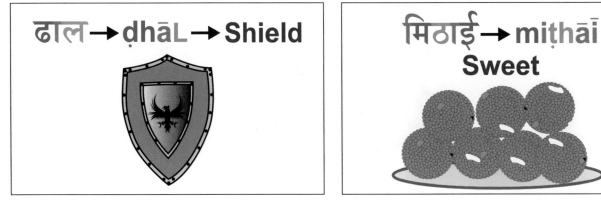

Fill in the blanks

Example: ko + nā = कोना

ḍhā + L = ____ल	chū + hā = ____हा
ḍa + r = ____र	jhī + L = ____ल
sū + kha + nā = ____खना	mī + ṭhā = मी____
be + cha + nā = ____चना	chhi + La + kā = ____लका
Li + fā + fā = लि____फा	ko + ya + L = ____यल

Match the following

ṭheLā	चेन	koyaL	ढपली
chen	ठेला	pāyaL	कोयल
miṭhāī	मीठा	ḍhapaLī	झरना
mīṭhā	मिठाई	jharanā	पायल
Lifāfā	डाकिया	ḍar	डरना
ḍākiyā	लिफाफा	ḍarnā	डर

Let's splash a bit of color!

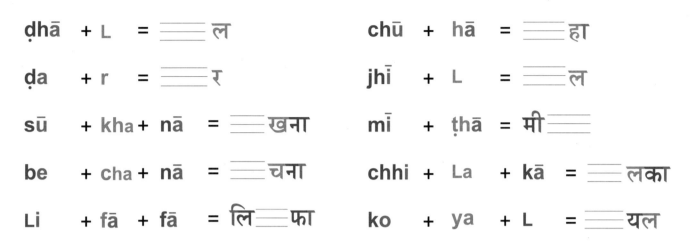

गुलाबी gulābī Pink

Reading

न	म	ग	ब	व	क	त	भ	प	च	छ	ज	र	ख	ल
na	ma	ga	ba	va	ka	ta	bha	pa	cha	chha	ja	ra	kha	La

स	श	फ	ट	य	ह	घ	द	थ	ध	ड	ढ	ठ	झ
sa	sha	pha, fa	ṭa	ya	ha	gha	da	tha	dha	ḍa	ḍha	ṭha	jha, za

आ	इ	ई	उ	ऊ	ए	ऐ	ओ	औ	अं
◌ा	ि◌	◌ी	◌ु	◌ू	◌े	◌ै	◌ो	◌ौ	◌ं ◌ँ
ā	i	ī	u	ū	e	ai	o	au	ń, ḿ

ढाल, झाग, ठाठ, पाठ, ढार, डाल

फाटक, नाटक, डगर, झालर, भाझर

ढीला, ढील, झील, ठीक, डीप, पीठ

ढोल, डोल, झोल, ठोक, टोक, ढकना, ठगना

ढोलक, डोकर, ठोकर, रोलर, मोटर,

रीना ढोलक बजाती है। खिलौने वाला आया। वह बहुत
सारे खिलौने लाया। ठेले पर बहुत सुंदर खिलौने है।
रीना जोर से पाठ पड़ती है। सब पतंग उड़ाते हैं।
फाटक बंद था। मेरे चाचा की शादी में ढोल बजा।
खाने के बरतन को ढकना चाहिए। ठोकर मत मार।
वे रोज झरना देखने जाते हैं। वे सब झील के
पास रहते है। मछली तालाब में तैरती हैं।
बाग में बहुत सारे पौधे लगे हैं। वहाँ बहुत सुंदर फूल है।
फूलों मे से खुशबू आती है। दादी गरम रोटी बनाती है।

This is quite fast,
I am almost there !

Go to page 6-7 and check

LESSON-10

Hey ! This is not rocket science !

Letters

ण

(ṇa) baṇd

ष

(sha) ṣhut

क्ष

(kṣha) workṣheet

त्र

(tra) thrash

ण	ṇa	baṇd
ष	ṣha	ṣhut
क्ष	kṣha	workṣheet
त्र	tra	thrash
ज्ञ	gya	harangue

ज्ञ

(gya) harangue

Letter Writing

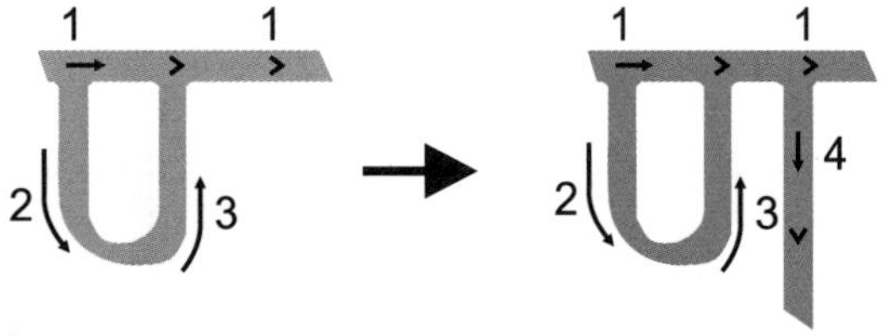

= ण (ṇa)

ण

ण

= ष (ṣh)

ष

ष

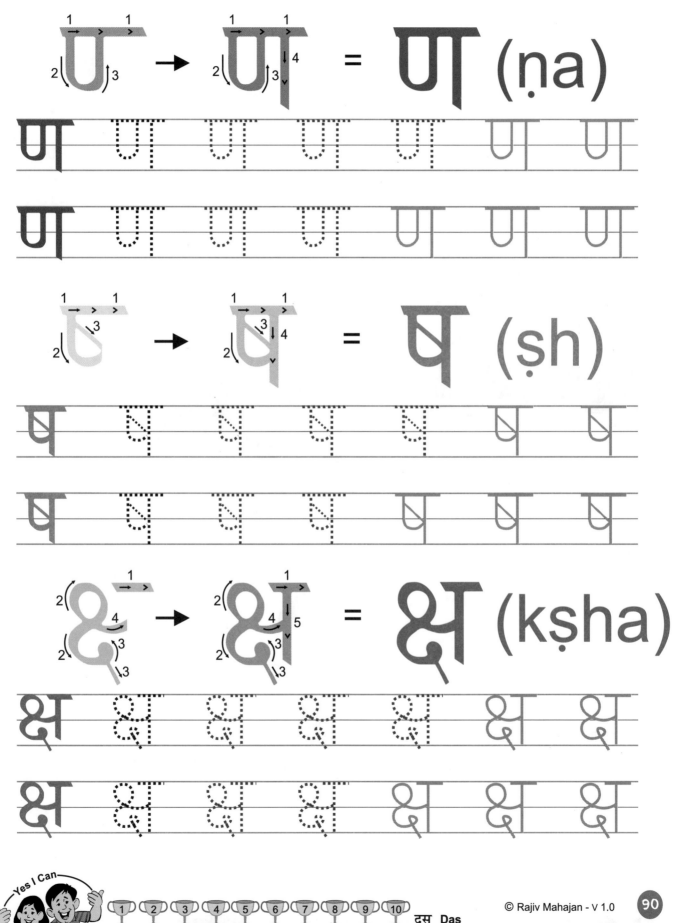

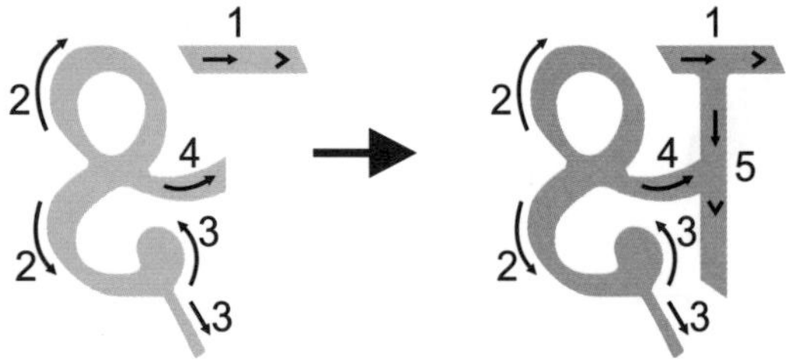

= क्ष (kṣha)

क्ष

क्ष

Letter Writing

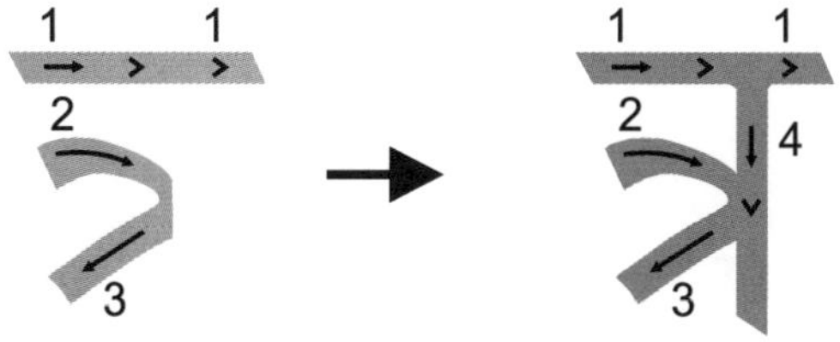

= त्र (tra)

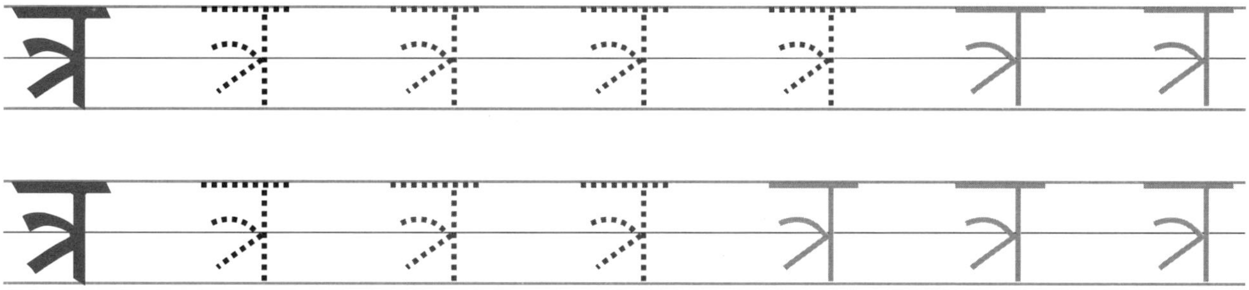

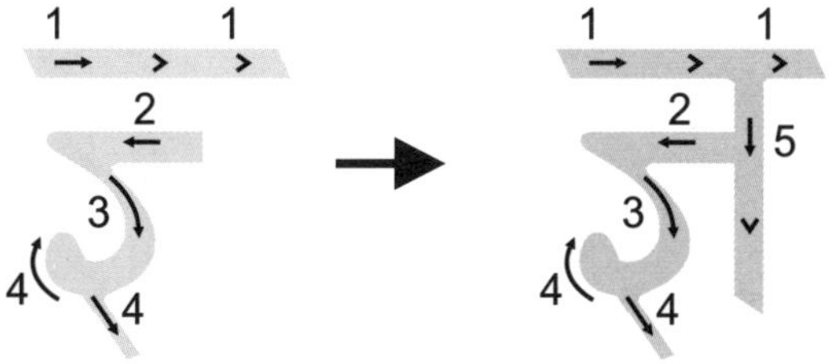

= ज्ञ (gya)

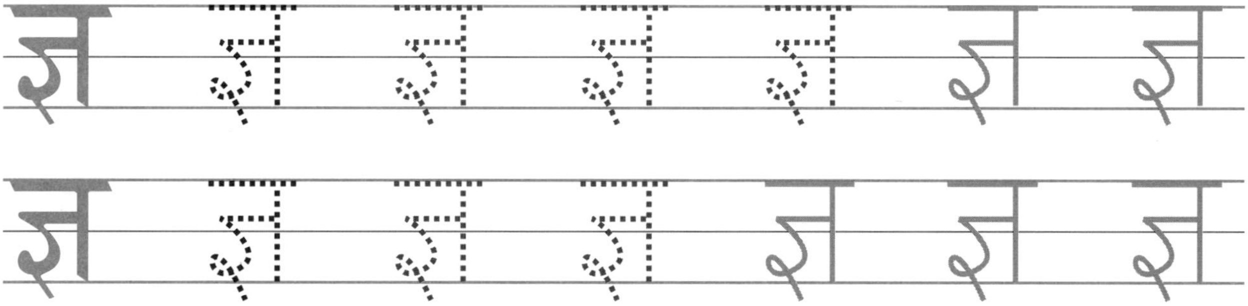

Let's go green with vegetables!

मिर्च mirch Chilli

Hindi Word Building

ि + श = शि

शि + क्ष + क = शिक्षक

shi + kṣha + k = shikṣhak **(Teacher)**

ब + ा = बा

बा + ण = बाण

bā + ṇ = bāṇ **(Arrow)**

भ + ा = भा

भा + ष + ण = भाषण

bhā + ṣha + ṇ = bhāṣhaṇ **(Speech)**

ि + म = मि

मि + त्र = मित्र

mi + tr = mitr **(Friend)**

प + क्ष + ी = पक्षी

pa + kṣh + ī = pakṣhī **(Bird)**

अ + क्ष + र = अक्षर

a + kṣha + r = akṣhar **(Alphabet)**

Build the following words

आ + ज्ञा = ______	शि + क्षा = ______
ज्ञा + न = ______	मा + त्रा = ______
द + क्षि + ण = ______	वि + शे + ष = ______
वि + ज्ञा + न = ______	रा + व + ण = ______
शो + ष + ण = ______	प + री + क्षा = ______

Combine the letters to form words

Example: ā + gyā = आज्ञा

ji + gyā + sā = ______	kā + ra + ṇ = ______
bhā + ṣhā = ______	shi + kṣhā = ______
vi + gyā + n = ______	gyā + nī = ______
ga + ṇe + ṣh = ______	da + kṣh = ______
ni + ṣhe + dh = ______	mo + kṣh = ______

Taste some fruits!

अनार anār Pomegranate

Word Meaning

चरण → charaṇ → Feet

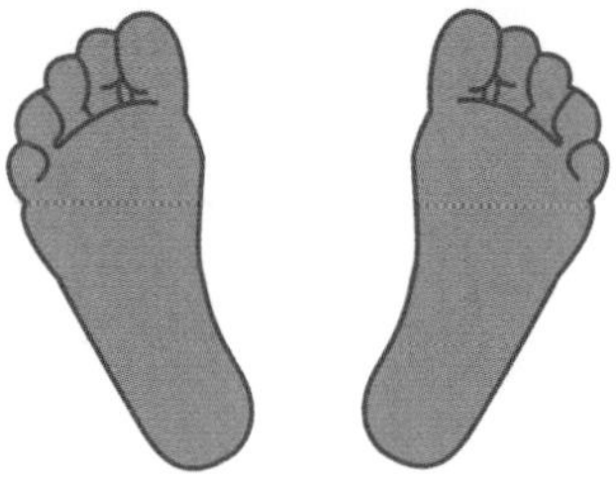

त्रिशूल → trishūL
Trident

त्रिभुज → tribhuj
Triangle

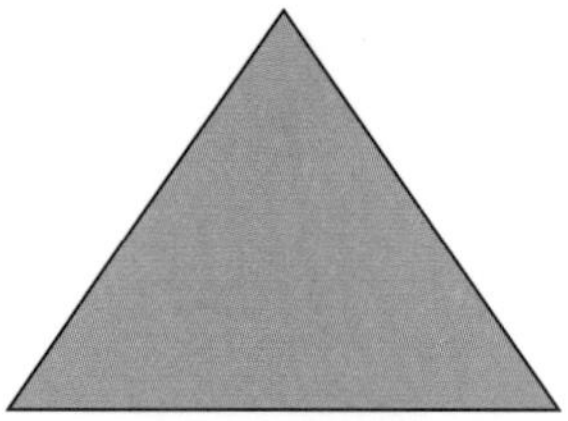

षटकोण → ṣhaṭkoṇ
Hexagon

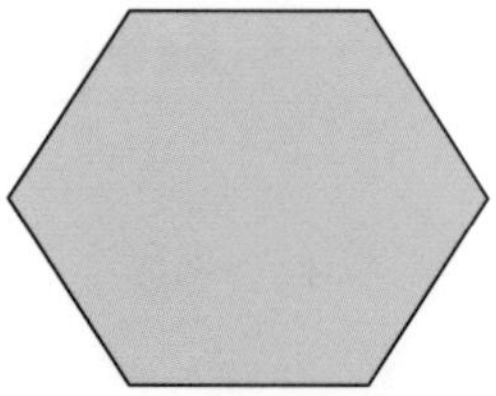

दक्षिण → dakṣhiṇ
South

भाषा → bhāṣhā
Language

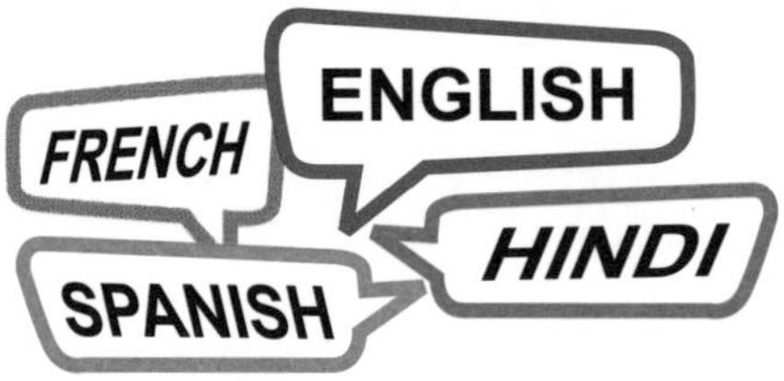

ज्ञान → gyān
knowledge

धनुष → dhanuṣh → Bow

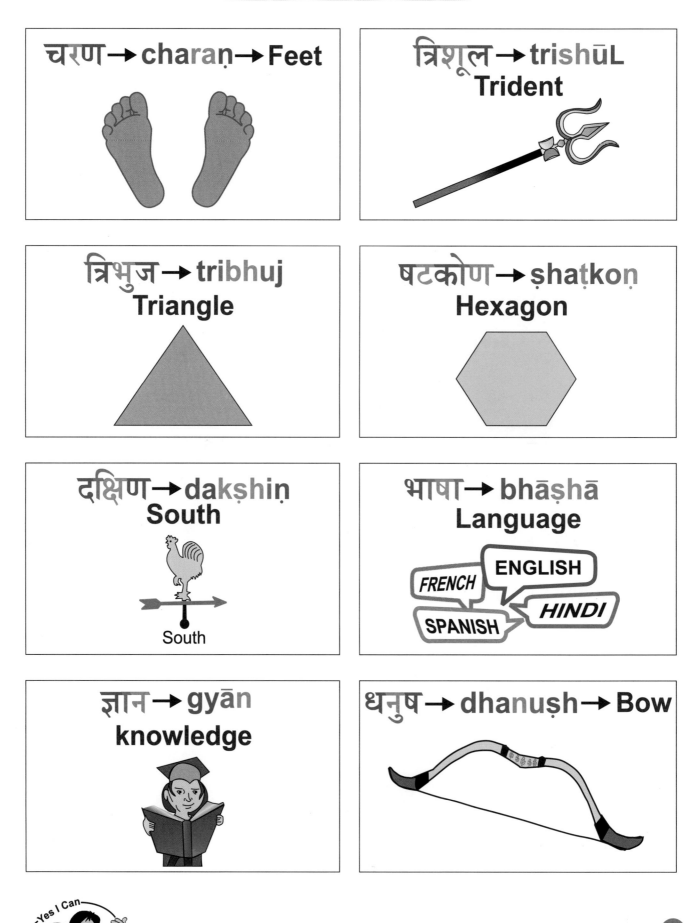

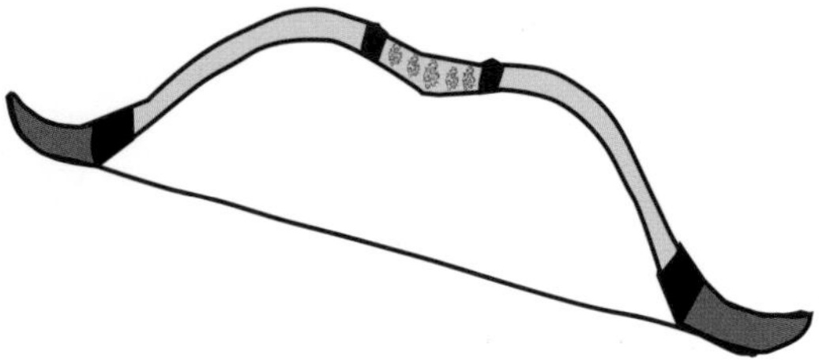

Fill in the blanks

Example: mā + trā = मात्रा

Bhā + Ṣhā	= भा ___		cha + ra + ṇ	= चर ___
gyā + n	= ___ न		pa + rī + kṣhā	= परी ___
vi + she + ṣh	= विशे ___		da + kṣhi + ṇ	= द ___ ण
ji + gyā + sā	= जि ___ सा		dha + nu + ṣh	= धनु ___
tri + shū + L	= ___ शूल		tri + bhu + j	= ___ भुज

Match the following

Bhāṣhā	त्रिशूल	charaṇ	मात्रा
trishūL	भाषा	kāraṇ	चरण
parīkṣhā	जिज्ञासा	mātrā	कारण
gyān	परीक्षा	dakṣhiṇ	शिक्षा
jigyāsā	विज्ञान	shikṣhā	पक्षी
vigyān	ज्ञान	pakṣhī	दक्षिण

Hey! What is this Vegetable called in Hindi?

कद्दू **kaddū Pumpkin**

Reading

न	म	ग	ब	व	क	त	भ	प	च	छ	ज	र	ख	ल	स	श
na	ma	ga	ba	va	ka	ta	bha	pa	cha	chha	ja	ra	kha	La	sa	sha

फ	ट	य	ह	घ	द	थ	ध	ड	ढ	ठ	झ	ण	ष	क्ष	त्र	ज्ञ
pha, fa	ṭa	ya	ha	gha	da	tha	dha	ḍa	ḍha	ṭha	jha, za	ṇa	ṣha	khṣa	tra	gya

आ	इ	ई	उ	ऊ	ए	ऐ	ओ	औ	अं
◌ा	ि◌	◌ी	◌ु	◌ू	◌े	◌ै	◌ो	◌ौ	◌ं ◌ँ
ā	i	ī	u	ū	e	ai	o	au	ń, ḿ

भाषा, आशा, ज्ञान, पासा, पात्र, छात्र

अज्ञान, पाषाण, मात्रा, छात्रा, दक्ष, पक्ष, लक्ष

त्रिभुज, त्रिशूल, पक्षी, राक्षस, रावण, कारण

शिक्षा, भिक्षा, अपेक्षा, कक्षा, आज्ञा

मीठा, चीटा, पीटा, टीका, फीका, हीरा, मीरा, खीरा

अनभिज्ञ, वनवासी, दशरथ, रामलीला, कबूतर

अब घर चल। देर मत कर। घर चल खाना बना।

पक्षी आकाश में उड़ते हैं। बतख पानी में चलती हैं।

अक्षर पर मात्रा लगा। तेज लिख। सुंदर लिख।

हमने सफेद कबूतर देखा। हम हिंदी लिखते हैं।

हमें हिंदी भाषा आती है। कक्षा में शोर मत कर।

अँगूर बहुत मीठे है। हीरा तेज चमकता है।

रावण जोर-जोर से हँसता है। गाय हरी घास खाती है।

गाय से हमें दूध मिलता है। आम फीका है।

दस Das

Yes. I could do it !

Don't forget to check on page 6-7

Supplement

Let's learn few more words before we complete this book !

Colors

Red
लाल LāL

Black
काला kāLā

White
सफ़ेद safed

Green
हरा harā

Yellow
पीला pīLā

Orange
संतरी sańtarī

Blue
नीला nīLā

Pink
गुलाबी guLābī

Brown
भूरा bhūrā

Gray
स्लेटी sLeṭī

Saffron
केसरिया kesariyā

Purple
बैंगनी baińganī

Golden
सुनहरा sunaharā

Silver
चाँदी chāńdī

Shiny
चमकीला chamakīLā

Numbers

Number	Hindi	Pronounce in Hindi
0	शून्य	shūnya
1	एक	ek
2	दो	do
3	तीन	tīn
4	चार	chār
5	पाँच	pāńch
6	छह	chhah
7	सात	sāt
8	आठ	āṭh
9	नौ	nau
10	दस	das
11	ग्यारह	gyārah
12	बारह	bārah
13	तेरह	terah
14	चौदह	chaudah
15	पंद्रह	pańdrah
16	सोलह	solah
17	सत्रह	satrah
18	अठारह	aṭhārah
19	उन्नीस	unnīs
20	बीस	bīs
21	इक्कीस	ikkīs
22	बाईस	bāīs
23	तेईस	teīs
24	चौबीस	chaubīs
25	पच्चीस	pachchīs
26	छब्बीस	chhabbīs
27	सत्ताईस	sattaīs
28	अठाईस	aṭhāīs
29	उन्नतीस	unnatīs
30	तीस	tīs
31	इक्कतीस	ikkatīs
32	बत्तीस	battīs

Number	Hindi	Pronounce in Hindi
33	तेंतीस	teńtīs
34	चौंतीस	chauńtīs
35	पैंतीस	paińtīs
36	छत्तीस	chhattīs
37	सैंतीस	saińtīs
38	अडतीस	aḍatīs
39	उनतालीस	unatāLīs
40	चालीस	chāLīs
41	इक्तालीस	iktāLīs
42	बयालीस	bayāLīs
43	तेंतालीस	taińtāLīs
44	चौवालीस	chauvāLīs
45	पैंतालीस	paińtāLīs
46	छियालीस	chhiyāLīs
47	सैंतालीस	saińtāLīs
48	अडतालीस	aḍatāLīs
49	उन्नचास	unnachās
50	पचास	pachās
51	इक्यावन	ikyāvan
52	बावन	bāvan
53	तिरेपन	tirepan
54	चौवन	chauvan
55	पचपन	pachapan
56	छप्पन	chhappan
57	सत्तावन	sattāvan
58	अठावन	aṭhāvan
59	उनसठ	unasaṭh
60	साठ	sāṭh
61	इकसठ	ikasaṭh
62	बासठ	bāsaṭh
63	तिरेसठ	tiresaṭh
64	चौंसठ	chauńsaṭh
65	पैंसठ	paińsaṭh
66	छियासठ	chhiyāsaṭh

Number	Hindi	Pronounce in Hindi
67	सडसठ	sadasaṭh
68	अडसठ	adasaṭh
69	उनहत्तर	unahattar
70	सत्तर	sattar
71	इकहत्तर	ikahattar
72	बहत्तर	bahattar
73	तिहत्तर	tihattar
74	चौहत्तर	chauhattar
75	पचहत्तर	pacahattar
76	छिहत्तर	chihattar
77	सतहत्तर	satahattar
78	अठहत्तर	aṭhahattar
79	उनासी	unāsī
80	अस्सी	assī
81	इक्यासी	ikyāsī
82	बयासी	bayāsī
83	तिरासी	tirāsī
84	चौरासी	chaurāsī
85	पचासी	pachāsī
86	छियासी	chhiyāsī
87	सत्तासी	sattāsī
88	अट्ठासी	aṭṭāsī
89	नवासी	navāsī
90	नब्बे	nabbe
91	इक्यानबे	ikyānabe
92	बानबे	bānabe
93	तिरानबे	tirānabe
94	चौरानबे	chaurānabe
95	पंचानबे	pańchānabe
96	छियानबे	chhiyānabe
97	सत्तानबे	sattānabe
98	अट्ठानबे	aṭṭānabe
99	निन्यानबे	ninyānabe
100	सौ	sau

Fruits

Apple
सेब
seb

Banana
केला
kelā

Grapes
अंगूर
ańgūr

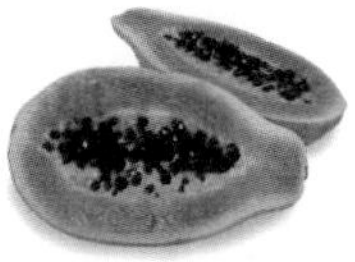
Papaya
पपीता
papītā

Black Berry
जामुन
jāmun

Sapodilla Plum
चीकू
chīckū

Custard Apple
शरीफा
sharīfā

Mango
आम
ām

Orange
संतरा
sańtarā

Pear
नाशपाती
nāshapātī

Plum
आलूभुखारा
ālūbhukhārā

Pineapple
अनानास
anānās

Pomegranate
अनार
anār

Water Melon
तरबूज
tarabūj

Wood Apple
बेल
beL

Guavas
अमरूद
amrūd

Chin Fruit
लीची
Līchī

Sweet Lime
मौसमी
mausamī

Dry Fruits

Walnuts
अखरोट
akharoṭ

Cashewnut
काजू
kājū

Dry Dates
खजूर
khajūr

Pistachio
पिस्ता
pistā

Raisins
किसमिस
kisamis

Apricot
खुमानी
khumānī

Figs
अंजीर
ańjīr

Vegetables

Potato
आलू
ālū

Tomato
टमाटर
ṭamāṭar

Onion
प्याज
pyāj

Carrot
गाजर
gājar

Radish
मूली
mūlī

Cabbage
पत्तागोभी
pattāgobhī

Cauliflower
फूलगोभी
fūlgobhī

Chilli
मिर्च
mirch

Coriander
धनिया
dhaniyā

Cucumber
खीरा
khīra

Bitter Gourd
करेला
karelā

Okara
भिन्डी
bhindī

Peas
मटर
maṭar

Colocasia
अरबी
arabī

Lotus stem
कमल ककडी
kamal kakadī

Pumpkin
कद्दू
kaddū

Spinach
पालक
pāLak

Cluster Beans
गुवारफली
guwārafaLī

Bell Pepper
शिमलामिर्च
shimalāmirch

Eggplant
बैंगन
baińgan

Ginger
अदरक
adarak

Human Body Parts

1. Skull
   खोपडी khopaḍī
2. Head
   सर sar
3. Hair
   बाल bāl
4. Face
   चेहरा cheharā
5. Forehead
   माथा māthā
6. Eye
   आँख āńkh
7. Eyebrow
   भौह bhauh
8. Eye lash
   पलक palak
9. Ear
   कान kān
10. Nose
    नाक nāk
11. Cheeks
    गाल gāl
12. Chin
    थोडी thoḍī
13. Neck
    गर्दन gardan

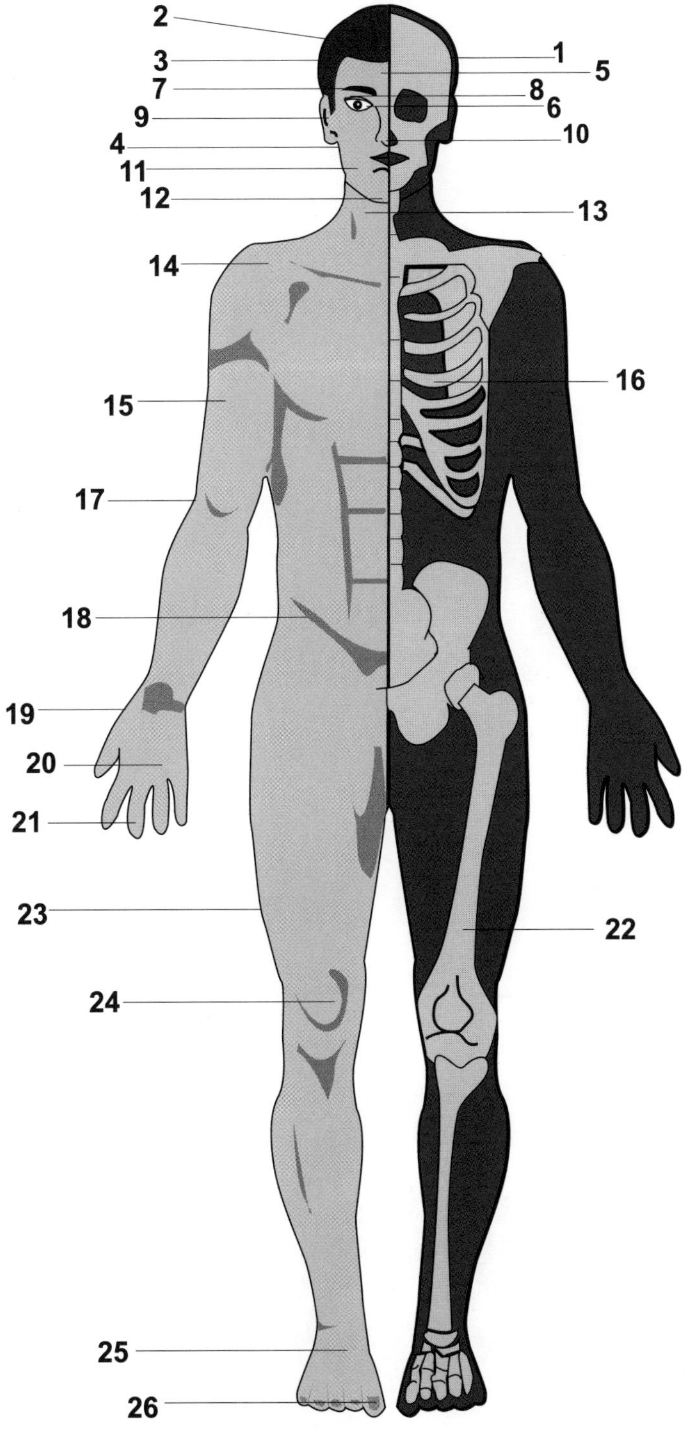

14. Shoulder
    कन्धा kandhā
15. Skin
    त्वचा twachā
16. Ribs
    पसली pasalī
17. Elbow
    कोहनी khohanī
18. Waist
    कमर kamar
19. Hand
    हाथ hāth
20. Palm
    हथेली hathelī
21. Finger
    ऊंगली ungalī
22. Bone
    हड्डी haḍḍī
23. Leg
    पैर pair
24. Knee
    घुटना ghuṭanā
25. Foot
    टांग ṭāńg
26. Nails
    नाखून nākhūn

Human Body Parts

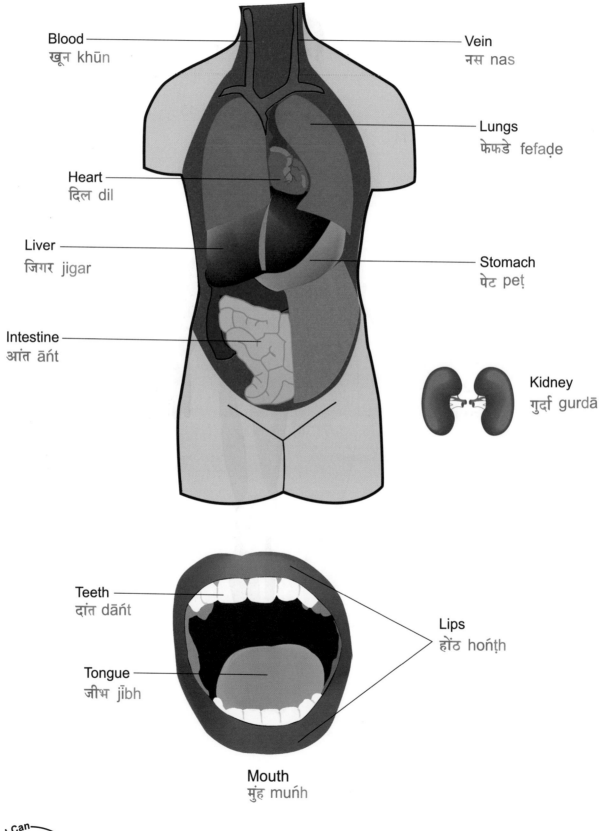

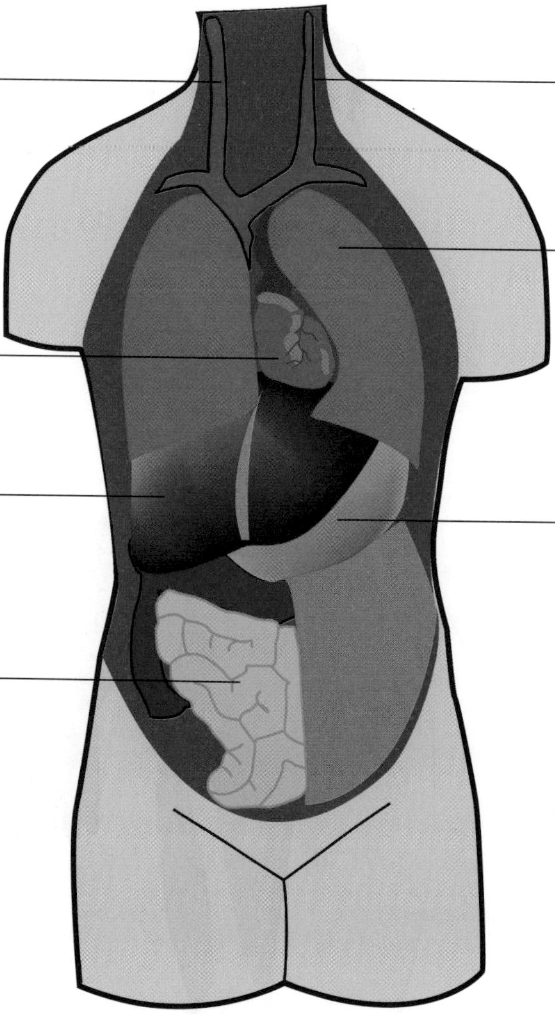
Blood
खून khūn
Vein
नस nas
Lungs
फेफडे fefaḍe
Heart
दिल dil
Liver
जिगर jigar
Stomach
पेट peṭ
Intestine
आंत āńt

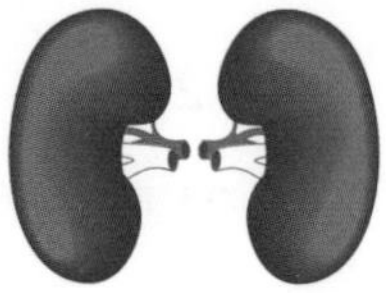
Kidney
गुर्दा gurdā

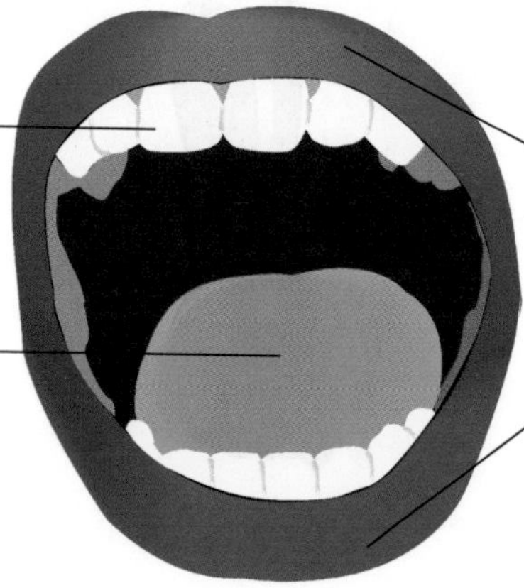
Teeth
दांत dāńt
Lips
होंठ hońṭh
Tongue
जीभ jībh
Mouth
मुंह muńh

The ABCD of Life

Life no doubt presents so many different challenges in front of us, at all times. While some of the solutions to these challenges get ingrained in our minds, others do not. My attempt through this set of 26 acronyms that I have compiled (representative of the 26 alphabets of the English language), is to help you remember various 'action-points' that you can take under diverse situations, as and when you face them.

You might be familiar with some of them – perhaps heard them before from others, while a few would probably be completely new to you. Either way, you could learn and imbibe these acronyms for future benefit. To make recall easier, I have tried my level best to include only those acronyms which are words by themselves, such as HOPE, MAGIC, etc.

I HOPE that the **MAGIC** of these acronyms will spread cheer in your **LIFE**, and bring joy to it.

- ABCD – Above and Beyond the Call of Duty
- BP – Be Positive
- CAP – Cover All Possibilities
- DIN – Do It Now
- ERIC – Emotional Reaction Impedes Control
- FEAR – False Evidence Appearing Real
- GREAT – Get Really Excited About Today
- HOPE – Helping Others Pursue Excellence
- ITALY – I Trust And Love You
- JAPAN – Just Always Pray At Night
- KISS – Kind In Self & Spirit
- LIFE – Living In Faith Everyday
- MAGIC – Miracles Always Greet Intensive Commitment
- NAMe - Not Always ME
- ONE – One Network for Everyone
- PURE – Purity Unleashes Remarkable Energy
- QuEst – Quality Establishment
- REAL – Realistic, Equal, & Active for Life
- STAR – Show Thankfulness, Appreciation & Respect
- TEAM – Together Everyone Achieves More
- USA – Unconditional Self Acceptance
- VIP – Victory In Prayer
- WIT – Whatever It Takes
- Xcel – Xcellence
- YOYO – You're On Your Own
- Z4L – Zeal 4 Life

Yes I did it !

Answers

Lesson 3

Combine the letters to form words (Pg. No. 29)

पिता → Father
मीना → Name of the person
माता → Mother
गिनना → Count
कीमत → Price
भाप → Steam
नापना → Measure
तीन → Three
भीगना → Getting wet
पपीता → Papaya

Fill in the blanks (Pg. No. 31)

पिन → Pin
मीना → Name of the person
पाप → Sin
पीना → To drink
गीता → Name of the person/ Holy Book
भाप → Steam
नापना → Measure
पपीता → Papaya
भवन → Building
गिनना → Count

Match the following (Pg. No. 31)

पीना → To drink
पानी → Water
पिता → Father
नाप → Measure
तीन → Three
मीना → Name of the person
गीता → Name of the person/ Holy Book
माता → Mother
भीगना → Getting wet
भवन → Building
पपीता → Papaya
पिन → Pin

Lesson 4

Combine the letters to form words (Pg. No. 38)

छूना → Touch
पूजा → Worship
चाबी → Key
नाजुक → Delicate
कछुआ → Turtle
चाकू → Knife
चूना → Kind of chemical
काजू → Cashew nut
नूतन → Newly
जुनून → Obsession

Fill in the blanks (Pg. No. 40)

पूजा → Worship
चुन → Choose
चुभ → Pinch
कछुआ → Turtle
नाजुक → Delicate
चाकू → Knife
काजू → Cashew nut
ऊन → Wool
नूतन → Newly
जुनून → Obsession

Match the following (Pg. No. 40)

चुप → Silence
छुप → Hide
जून → June (Month Name)
कछुआ → Turtle
जीभ → Tongue
काजू → Cashew nut
छूना → Touch
बाजू → Arms
पूजा → Worship
चीनी → Sugar

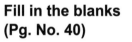

Lesson 5

Combine the letters to form words (Pg. No. 47)

खेत → Farm
मेला → Fair
रेत → Sand
चेन → Chain
जेलर → Warden
आलू → Potato
रानी → Queen
गैर → Non
मैला → Muddy

Fill in the blanks (Pg. No. 49)

रेन → Rain
मैप → Map
मेल → Mail
जेलर → Warden
वैन → Van/Car
जैम → Jam
रेल → Train
जेल → Prison
केवल → Only
खेलना → Play

Match the following (Pg. No. 49)

जैम → Jam
जेल → Prison
रेत → Sand
कलम → Pen
छत → Roof
नेपाल → Name of country
पागल → Mad
रेन → Rain
खेलना → Play
केवल → Only
रेल → Train
तैरना → Swim

(Note: चेन, रेन, मैप, मेल, जैम – All these words are not Hindi words)

Lesson 6

Combine the letters to form words (Pg. No. 56)

खोज → Search
भालू → Bear
शोर → Noise
पैर → Leg
बकरी → Goat
मोरनी → Peahen
पौना → Three quarter
शौक → Hobby
बारिश → Rain
नौकर → Servant
सूरज → Sun

Fill in the blanks (Pg. No. 58)

बोल → Lyrics
सोना → Gold/To sleep
चोर → Thief
मोर → Peacock
कानून → Law
पोशाक → Dress/Outfit
खोज → Search
फूल → Flower
गोल → Circular
बोलना → Speak
लिखना → Write

Match the following (Pg. No. 58)

चोर → Thief
कौआ → Crow
पोशाक → Dress/Outfit
मोरनी → Peahen
बोलना → Speak
खिलौना → Toy
मेज → Table
सोना → Gold/To sleep
फूल → Flower
औरत → Lady
गिलास → Glass
खोजना → Search

Lesson 7

Combine the letters to form words (Pg. No. 65)

पँख → Wing
जंग → War/Rust
हीरा → Diamond
खीरा → Cucumber
तितली → Butterfly
तरंग → Wave
फाँसी → To be hanged/Gallows
कटोरी → Bowl
टोकरी → Basket
फँसना → Getting Caught
जंगल → Forest

Fill in the blanks (Pg. No. 67)

टोपी → Cap
चूहा → Rat
तौलिया → Towel
तितली → Butterfly
बोतल → Bottle
बहुत → Very
ताला → Lock
खिलौना → Toy
बिजली → Power/Electricity
तराजू → Weighing balance
टहनी → Tree Branch

Match the following (Pg. No. 67)

मयूर → Peacock
जंग → War/Rust
ताला → Lock
बुक → Book
बीमार → *Ill*
युवक → Youth
बहुत → Very
तिरंगा → National Flag of India
रंग → Color
टोपी → Cap
तितली → Butterfly

(Note: बुक - not a Hindi word)

Lesson 8

Combine the letters to form words (Pg. No. 74)

दुख → Sorrow
धूप → Sunshine
दूध → Milk
घर → Home
पुदीना → Mint
गरमी → Heat/Summer
दादी → Grand mother
दिया → Gave
खीरा → Cucumber
धरती → Earth
पुजारी → Priest

Fill in the blanks (Pg. No. 76)

धूप → Sunshine
जाप → Recite (Pray)
दुख → Sorrow
धन → Money/Wealth
घूमना → Stroll/Revolve
धरती → Earth
रस्सी → Rope
थाली → Plate
धागा → Thread
दीवार → Wall
दुकान → Shop

Match the following (Pg. No. 76)

दुख → Sorrow
दूध → Milk
थाली → Plate
माली → Gardner
दीवार → Wall
दीया → Lamp
दीपक → Lamp
दुकान → Shop
घर → Home
धागा → Thread
दादी → Grand mother
घूमना → Stroll/Revolve

(Note: रोप - not a Hindi word)

Lesson 9

Combine the letters to form words (Pg. No. 83)

ठग → Thug
राजा → King
खोना → Lose
पीसना → Grind
लिफाफा → Envelope
सुनना → Listen
देना → Give
लेना → Take
पुदीना → Mint
भूलना → Forget
डूबना → Sink

(Note: चेन - not a Hindi word)

Fill in the blanks (Pg. No. 85)

कोना → Corner
ढाल → Gradient
डर → Fear
सूखना → Dry
बेचना → Sell
लिफाफा → Envelope
चूहा → Rat
झील → Lake
मीठा → Sweet
छिलका → Skin/Outer layer
कोयल → Cuckoo

Match the following (Pg. No. 85)

ठेला → Barrow/Cart
चेन → Chain
मिठाई → Sweets
मीठा → Sweet
लिफाफा → Envelope
डाकिया → Postman
कोयल → Cuckoo
पायल → Anklet
ढपली → Tambourine/Drum
झरना → Waterfall
डर → Fear
डरना → To fear

Lesson 10

Combine the letters to form words (Pg. No. 93)

आज्ञा → Permission
जिज्ञासा → Desire
भाषा → Language
विज्ञान → Science
गणेश → Name of God
निषेध → Negation/Prohibition
कारण → Reason
शिक्षा → Education
ज्ञानी → Wise person
दक्ष → Expert
मोक्ष → Salvation

Fill in the blanks (Pg. No. 95)

मात्रा → Quantity
भाषा → Language
ज्ञान → Knowledge
विशेष → Important
जिज्ञासा → Desire
त्रिशूल → Trident
चरण → Feet
परीक्षा → Exam
दक्षिण → South
धनुष → Bow
त्रिभुज → Triangle

Match the following (Pg. No. 95)

भाषा → Language
त्रिशूल → Trident
परीक्षा → Exam
ज्ञान → Knowledge
जिज्ञासा → Desire
विज्ञान → Science
चरण → Feet
कारण → Reason
मात्रा → Quantity
दक्षिण → South
शिक्षा → Education
पक्षी → Bird

Certificate

Congratulations to

....

you have completed the Let's Begin Level 1 of

Yes. I can Read, Write & Speak Hindi Series

and are now ready for level 2.

Teacher:........................ Date:......................